LONG LIVE
THE
QUEEN MARY!

C.W.R. WINTER

Whippingham, Isle of Wight, England

Published by Forget-Me-Not Books and The Manor Design & Printing Partnership.

ISBN 1 870374 25 8 (De Luxe Edition)
ISBN 1 870374 30 4 (Hardback)

Produced by The Manor Design & Printing Partnership, Whitwell, Isle of Wight, England.

By the same author:
Queen Mary: Her Early Years Recalled
The Ancient Town of Yarmouth
The Manor Houses of the Isle of Wight
Village Churches of the Isle of Wight
The Run of the Tide
Travellers Joy
The Enchanted Isle

Contents

Acknowledgements

Most authors are proud to claim that the book they are presenting is all their own work . I am even more proud to say that this book *"Long Live the Queen Mary!"* is not all my own work, for many good people have contributed to it, not only in writing but with ideas, suggestions and general encouragement.

I am particularly grateful to all those who accepted my invitation to write about their own individual involvement with the *Queen Mary,* and Chapters 12 to 25 which are the result, are exciting, refreshing, and indicative of the widespread devotion to this extraordinary old lady.

But I must mention one or two people who have been especially kind, firstly in helping to put this book together, but also in the wider sense of supporting the object of the book, which is the preservation of the *Queen Mary.* I think particularly of George Kean, both for his contribution and for reminding us that in Clydebank they not only built ships, they built friendships. In a world torn apart by squabbling men this statement is a rock on which we can build further. I mention also Hal Johnson for the tireless work he and many others did in the dark days in 1992 when the future of the ship looked very bleak. Their steadfastness and fortitude did much to save her, and will not be forgotten.

But my greatest thanks go to two people. Diane Rush, President of the *Queen Mary* Foundation, who has contributed Chapters 6 and 7 and has demonstrated, perhaps to the amazement of some people, what dedication is all about. She has consistently put the welfare of the ship before her own career, and the *Queen Mary* is indeed fortunate to have her as a devotee.

And finally David Hutchings. What can I say about David except to remind you that he is a well known author in his own right and yet he has unstintingly helped with this present book. David has supplied many of the illustrations herein, including the delightful cartoon character *'Mac',* the Scottish ships engineer, who appears throughout, and I am indeed most grateful to him.

Together we say - "Long Live the *Queen Mary!"*

Foreword

by Commodore Geoffrey T. Marr, D.S.C., R.D., Cmdr R.N.R. (Ret'd)

It was only when it was suggested that I might write the Foreword to Ron Winter's fascinating book, *"Long Live the Queen Mary"*, that I fully realised how closely my career at sea had been integrated with this wonderful ship.

It was in 1936, the year when in which she made her maiden voyage, that I first joined the Cunard White Star Line. But it was not until 1938, when I was sent down from Liverpool to Southampton to join her, as a Junior Third Officer, that I saw her for the first time. This proved an unforgettable experience. As I got out of my taxi, close to her enormous bow which towered sixty feet above me, and gazed in awe at her staggering bulk – *"Long as a street, and lofty as a block of flats"* – my heart sank as I thought, however does one learn how to handle anything as big as this?

Well, at various times during the next thirty years I was to sail her, in every different Officer's rank, as I slowly climbed the promotion ladder, and during some of those periods I was to have some of the happiest, and some more alarming, experiences, as I have told in my own autobiography *"The Queens and I"*, published in 1973.

When I finally retired from the Cunard Line in 1968, it was only a few months after Captain John Treasure Jones had berthed her successfully in Long Beach to start an entirely new life.

During my retirement I have followed her career with great interest, firstly, from my close personal friendship with her last Captain, then later, through the good offices of the *Queen Mary* Foundation. But I must confess that I have learned many more facts from reading this fascinating book, than I ever new before, and can only hope that its sales will help to prolong the life of this wonderful ship.

But I should like to use words of more eloquence than mine to pay tribute to this great ship, by repeating those of an American writer, Noel Mostert, who said in his *"Farewell to the Great Ships"*:

"The two older 'Queens' undoubtedly will always remain the finest ships ever built. No matter how large those giant super-tankers grow, and they are building today 500,000 tonners, which will be a third again as long as a 'Queen'. Because no tanker, no matter what size, could ever carry the visual impact of those two magnificent ships. Especially when seen at speed, flinging the North Atlantic aside, in huge combers. Their whole line one of power and splendour, Oceanic Palaces of staggering dimensions."

Commodore Geoffrey Marr, D.S.C., R.D.,
Cmdr R.N.R. (Retd.)

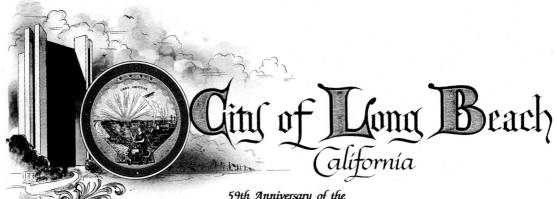

City of Long Beach
California

59th Anniversary of the
Launch of the Queen Mary in
Clydebank, Scotland
September 26, 1993

Whereas, the cities of Clydebank, Scotland and Long Beach, California share in common a substantial interest in the historic ship Queen Mary; and

Whereas, the Queen Mary, presently moored in the City of Long Beach, California, was built in Clydebank, Scotland and launched on September 26, 1934; and

Whereas, in celebration of this anniversary, several persons involved in the building and launch of the Queen Mary will be aboard the ship to commemorate this event. Most notably present will be:

John Brown
Chief Architect and Designer of the Queen Mary

George Kean
Shipwright who helped build the Queen Mary

C.W.R. (Ron) Winter
Junior Electrician on board the Queen Mary from 1936-1939
Author of The Queen Mary, Her Early Years Recalled;

Also attending will be:

Alistair McDonald, Provost
Clydebank, Scotland

Mr. Jack Webster
Scottish Journalist and Editor
Glasgow Herald;

Whereas, the City of Clydebank also shares in common with Long Beach its shipyards, its location as a Port City, and its interest in expanding people-to-people friendship with other cities;

Now, Therefore, I, Ernie Kell, Mayor of the City of Long Beach, congratulate the efforts of those celebrating this 59th Anniversary of the launch of the historic ship Queen Mary and proclaim September 26, 1993 as **Long Beach-Clydebank Friendship Day** in the City of Long Beach.

Ernie Kell
M A Y O R

Dated: September 26, 1993

Chapter 1

In the Beginning

There is no doubt that the *Queen Mary* exercises an extraordinary and compelling fascination over a great number of people, and it is not impossible, nor even too difficult, to see the reason why. All ships have an attraction to some degree, possibly because they enable us to contend with a strange and often hostile environment, the sea, and also because many of them have a rather pleasant shape and are good to look upon.

This latter attraction is not the only attribute that a ship shares with a woman, and men have been known to become just as obsessed with the one as with the other. Indeed, psychiatrists tell us that every tender feeling a man has is in some way sublimated sex, though this is perhaps taking the argument to the verge of embarrassment. Let it suffice that ships have a definitely feminine quality which makes them curiously appealing, not only to men but also to women, and this attraction can lead to a blind, and lifelong devotion.

But the *Queen Mary* exercises her own particular magic in the feelings she inspires. Maybe this is in part due to her enormous size and the fact that she was so cunningly designed that she does not appear overlarge. In many ways she has the graceful lines of a yacht, and her beauty of form not only conceals her tremendous bulk but also, nowadays, her age. Perhaps the ability to look younger than she is can be regarded as another fairly common feminine quality, to achieve which many women go to enormous lengths.

Maybe also it is due to her illustrious parentage, for she comes of a long line of splendid Cunard ships stretching way back to their original Britannia in 1840. With such names among your forbears as *Aquitania, Mauritania, Berengaria,* and *Lusitania* it must surely be that you have indeed been born into the elite, and can expect to be treated with deference and respect. We must also never forget her somewhat unusual birth, for this is without doubt another of the ingredients that give her such a special quality.

She was conceived in the midst of a recession, at a time when the shipping industry was in the doldrums and no one in their right mind was building ships. It was an outrageous concept, a courageously bold and visionary idea in those circumstances, this plan to build two ships, so large, so fast, and so reliable that they could between them do the work of three ships and sustain a regular weekly ferry service between Europe and America. It was perhaps typical of the Cunard company, who had built up a reputation on the North Atlantic second to none, and who realised that if this dream could be turned into reality it would establish their supremacy over their competitors for many years to come.

Following conception the gestation period was not without its problems. Almost exactly a year after the keel was laid money ran out and work was stopped. We, at this distance in time, and sitting in our comfortable homes, cannot possibly imagine the depth of depression that settled over Clydeside. The placing of the order for No. 534 had seemed like the answer to their prayers, for poverty and near starvation was rife on Clydebank, and some of the most skilled shipbuilders in the world had been finding it difficult to survive. And to have this Godsend of an order snatched away from them only a year later must have been a blow very hard to bear.

For over two years Clydesiders had the mortification of seeing the semi-completed hull of No. 534 standing idle on the ways. During this period many prophets of gloom and doom shook their heads and expressed the view that it may have been a very beautiful dream, but that it was only a dream, and one that would never come true. They prophesied that in due course we should find her plating being taken away to be used on smaller and more practical jobs, and that No. 534 would quietly be written off.

Thankfully they were wrong, and in April 1934 work resumed, following the merger of Cunard with White Star and the subsequent Government financial help. The enthusiasm with which this event was greeted on Clydeside was unparalleled, and it spread far and wide, beyond the Clyde, beyond the Scottish borders, until ultimately it reached even the furthest parts of the British Empire.

Every country in the Empire wanted to be part of this ship, to contribute something towards her, and as a result she became truly a British ship, a product of many diverse cultures and skills.

The Empire, for example, provided over fifty varieties of beautiful woods, and the richness and profusion of the veneers in her

Lady Hilton's Marble Plaque of H.M. Queen Mary (University Archives, University of Liverpool).

public rooms and private cabins became an outstanding feature of the ship, a feature that we can still enjoy today. As it was being fitted, all the panelling was backed by flannel so that when the ship was working in a seaway there should be no creaking, a problem that besets many passenger ships. This is a typical example of the trouble taken to ensure that she should be as near perfect as possible.

All these ingredients contributed to making her the greatest ship of her time, and one that caught and captured the attention of the whole world. There are those who maintain that the French Line's *Normandie* was a more beautiful ship and her decor more dazzling and imaginative than that of the *Queen Mary*, and no one can deny the *Normandie's* claim to fame, but as a ship, a practical yet beautiful device for transporting men and women in comfort across one of the most capricious of oceans, the *Queen Mary* has no equal. In a souvenir booklet produced at the time of her maiden voyage in May 1936, the writer E.P. Leigh-Bennett had this to say -

"The essence of her beauty lies in her extreme utility for the many purposes of the sea. Bizarre settings and grotesquely sumptuous trappings, foreign to the British temperament, find no place in her. Brilliance of conception appears everywhere in her adornment. Through all the interior acres devoted to practical uses, the prevailing impression is of forthright British comfort, without question of expense. Having watched her grow, slowly but very surely, from keel to funnels over the years, and then having wandered (for miles) about her over the weeks, while 250,000 men and women, in over eighty British cities and towns, were busy upon her myriad needs, I realise thankfully, as all who see her will, how immutable still is this country's sense of quality when left unimpeded to produce the best."

Once work had resumed it proceeded at an ever increasing pace, for there was much to be done to prepare the hull for launching. One shipwright who remembers these days well is George Kean, who was 17 years old at the time. George had served his apprenticeship in John Brown's Yard and worked both on No.

534 and later on No. 552, *Queen Mary*'s sister ship *Queen Elizabeth*. This is what he says about the day the *Queen Mary* was launched.

"*On the 26th September 1934 I woke to the sound of bells ringing in my ears. It was my trusty alarm clock telling me it was time to go to my work in John Brown's Shipyard in Clydebank. I got up and looked out of the window. It was raining cats and dogs, coming down in buckets as we say. I heard my mum calling from the kitchen that my porridge was getting cold. She kept telling me that porridge was good, it sticks to your ribs and keeps the cold out. As I entered the kitchen my mum reminded me this was the day I was to meet King George and Queen Mary who were to launch Ship No. 534, the largest ship in the world. It was still dark and 6.30 a.m.*

I donned my overalls and macintosh and made my way through driving rain, hardly a soul about. When I reached the main road leading to the yard I was amazed at the sight of hun-

No. 534 takes shape (University Archives, University of Glasgow).

dreds of well dressed people under a multitude of umbrellas of all colours making their way to the launch to get a good vantage point, and this was over eight hours to launch time. I had to go through a special gate to sign on. My job was with a squad of shipwrights to take away strategic blocks below the ship until the last minute so that it would be left for a few minutes held by twelve electrically controlled triggers. So everything had to be done to a tight programme.

Just after 2 p.m. we heard a mighty roar from the crowd as the Royal Party approached the launch platform, and we had a good view of them. Our foreman came round with sweets which was a very old custom. Imagine free sweets and wages too! Soon the speeches started and we had only six sets of wood blocks to remove. The King started speaking and introduced his Queen. Just then we noticed that the ship had moved imperceptibly as data plates had parted on the static and moveable launchways. We

were told to get out and leave the blocks and as we got into the open we heard the Queen saying "I name this ship Queen Mary" and the rest was drowned out by the cheering and shouting. It seemed to be a popular choice. The Queen struck the block and the ship slid away into the mist.

There was a terrific noise from the thousands of tons of steel cables attached to each side of the ship to slow it down as it reached its natural environment. A huge wave was produced as she entered the water and people on both sides of the river Clyde were drenched even more than they had been. The chains finally stopped the ship right in the middle of the river and eight busy tugs soon had her in tow and neatly manoeuvred her into the fitting basin where she remained for another two years.

I last saw R.M.S. Queen Mary when she left in March 1936 for her maiden voyage. I had first entered the huge hull in 1932 at 15 years of age, and when she left I was almost a fully fledged shipwright. I was sorry to see

September 26, 1934. A day to remember. (University Archives, University of Liverpool).

Fitting Out – and jutting out. (David F. Hutchings).

her go. You see, in Clydebank we not only built ships, we built friendships."

George Kean spoke these words on 26th September 1993, the 59th Anniversary of this memorable occasion in which he played a vital part. He was speaking in the main first class lounge of the ship he had helped to build, to an assembled company of visitors who had come to celebrate this unique anniversary. I was privileged also to speak on this occasion and was sitting next to him, while on his other side was John Brown, who as a young naval architect, had had the responsibility of interpreting the Cunard White Star Directors' dream and committing it to paper. You can imagine what this occasion meant to all of us, and I shall refer to the anniversary ceremony again later on.

Perhaps the hiccough in the early history of the ship accounts for the particular pride and affection felt by all who worked on her, a pride shared by all the hundreds of firms who were involved in fitting her out. Typical was the attitude of one West Country carpet

manufacturer who had been weaving hand-tufted carpets since 1701, but who regarded their order for the *Queen Mary* as one of their greatest honours.

But long before carpets could be laid came the launch, and the date of 26th September had been chosen with meticulous care for, on this day, a spring tide was anticipated, and the ship's designers were very conscious of her great draught, and the comparative shallowness of the Clyde River. Two years later, in March 1936, when she was ready to leave Clydebank, and her draught was considerably greater than when she was launched, they were to face the same situation again and this problem with the tides.

The presence of the King and Queen made the launch ceremony a Royal Occasion, and in

THE 'QUEEN SEEMS TO BRING OUT THE ARTIST IN SOME PEOPLE!

Above: *Nearly ready for sea.* (David F. Hutchings).
Below: *Down the River Clyde to the future.* (Elliot Hamilton).

fact it was the first time a reigning sovereign had officiated on such an occasion. There had been great speculation as to what the ship's name would be, and the secret had been well kept, but apart from the bookmakers who possibly lost money on the bets that had been placed, I do not think many people were unhappy when the Queen graciously gave No. 534 her own name.

The tens of thousands of cheering Clydesiders present made the heavens echo as she slid down the ways, for they could now see their dream coming true. Her launching weight was a staggering 40,000 tons, an enormous mass to handle from high on the land down into the water, but the launch was carried out without a hitch, and she came to rest in the river within a foot of the position calculated by the engineers. She was at this stage of course an empty shell without fittings of any kind, and from then on began the task of fitting her out.

First were the 24 Yarrow water tube boilers to provide steam for her propulsion, together with the 3 Scotch boilers and plant for producing electric power and light. Then the massive steam turbines themselves together with all the other ancillary machinery necessary, and hundreds of miles of pipework and cables. All this equipment and machinery was of the very highest quality, the finest that Britain could produce, and in the 1930's that meant the best in the world. Now, in the 1990's, when practically the whole of her machinery has been stripped out and demolished, sold for scrap, let us pause for a moment and consider just what has been lost.

Chapter 2

The Nuts and Bolts

Once the decision had been taken to build two ships capable of maintaining a regular weekly service between Europe and America, and specifically between Southampton, Cherbourg and New York, the exciting business of designing the first ship began. A matter of primary importance was the choice of propelling machinery, for the method of propulsion has a considerable bearing on the design of the ship as a whole, since it affects the arrangement of the passenger accommodation. As well as the comfort of the passengers, reliability and economy have to be carefully considered.

There were several schools of thought as to the most suitable type of propulsion, and a not surprising divergence of opinion between the use of diesel engines and steam turbines. Since the dramatic introduction of the Parsons turbine engined ship *Turbinia* at Queen Victoria's Diamond Jubilee review of the Fleet in 1897, steam turbines had steadily displaced reciprocating steam engines and were the front runners. But diesel engines had made great progress too, and were by many thought to be the engines of the future. Cunard were determined to find the best solution, and early in 1929 invited a number of leading British marine engineers to serve in an honorary capacity on a Committee to discuss the problem and advise.

This Committee, among whose members were Sir Charles Parsons himself and a young John Austin who, as Chief Superintendent Engineer, played such a vital part in ensuring the success of the machinery installation, deliberated long and seriously. They decided that the most important considera-tion by far was reliability, and that this was followed fairly closely by quietness of operation, both these requirements being essential in a passenger liner whose amenities had to include those of a first class hotel as well as being propelled across the Atlantic at high speed. Breakdowns, noise, and vibration were simply unacceptable. Only after these requirements had been satisfied did they turn their attention to the very important subject of fuel consumption and other economies which would have a profound influence on the successful trading operations as a ship.

After considering all these points the Committee's recommendation to the Board was that they should adopt high pressure, high temperature steam driving single reduction geared turbines as the main propulsion units. The Board accepted this recommendation, and were then in a position to invite tenders for the construction of the first ship, and this was duly given to John Brown's Clydebank Shipyard which had a long history of the successful manufacture of many Cunarders and warships.

As the design developed it was soon realised that to provide the power required an enormous amount of steam would be needed, and ultimately 24 Yarrow water tube boilers of advanced design were installed. These were capable of producing steam at over 400 pounds per square inch pressure and at a temperature of 700 degrees

Fahrenheit, and it is useful to try and imagine what these figures mean.

A pressure of 400 lbs/sq.in.. is nearly four times higher than the pressure of air we use in our motor car tyres and is a very high pressure indeed. And to imagine how hot 700 degrees Fahrenheit is we have to remember that water boils at 212 degrees and this is nearly three and a half times hotter than that. Incidentally, a scale model of one of these incredible boilers is on show in the *Queen Mary's* Exhibition Hall, and though it is in a glass case and not operating, it is in fact a working model and is quite capable of producing steam at the figures quoted above. What is more, it has been designed to work on exactly the same fuel, Bunker C, as the original full size boilers, which says much for the skill of its designer and builder, Robin Jacobs.

The turbines, which all this steam was produced to drive, were interesting too. The *Queen Mary* had four propellers to push her along, each one on its own shaft and driven by its own engine. Each engine consisted of four turbines, all driving the one shaft through a large gear wheel. The reason for four turbines is to make use of every scrap of pressure and temperature in the steam that comes from the boilers.

The steam first enters the High Pressure Turbine and turns this, as you can imagine, at some speed. When it leaves this turbine it has lost some of its pressure and temperature, and is then fed into the First Intermediate Pressure Turbine. In turning this turbine it loses a little more pressure and temperature, and then goes to the Second Intermediate Pressure stage where the same process is carried on. The fourth turbine is called the Low Pressure Turbine, for by this time the steam has lost a lot of its zing and is feeling pretty tired, though it still has enough energy left to turn this low pressure machine.

But when the steam leaves the low pressure stage it is literally exhausted and has lost all its energy. So there is only one thing to be done with it, and this is to pass it through a Condenser which will turn it back into water, and it can then be returned to the boilers and used again. Which means that very little of the precious fresh water is wasted. A condenser, incidentally, is a very simple device in principle. Basically it is a tank of cold water through which pass a

Scotch Boilers in No.1 Boiler Room. Steam for the Generators. (University Archives, University of Liverpool).

large number of small pipes carrying the exhausted steam. These pipes are surrounded by circulating cold sea water, which effectively turns the steam back into water.

As you may well imagine, in practice the engines are slightly more complicated than the above simple explanation may suggest, and a whole host of auxiliary machinery was necessary to make them work. For instance, in the *Queen Mary's* engine rooms there were dozens of pumps of different sizes, air pumps, fresh water pumps, sea water pumps,

Above: *After Engine Room Starting Platform. Still preserved today.* (University Archives, University of Liverpool).

Top left: *Three 1300KW Generators. Electricity for the Hotel services.* (University Archives, University of Liverpool).

Left: *No.5 Boiler Room. Steam at over 400p.s.i. for the Main Propulsion Turbines.* (University Archives, University of Liverpool).

oil fuel pumps, boiler feed pumps, lubricating oil pumps, etc., etc., over sixty of them in all. Some were very large, and among these were the fans used to pump air into the boiler rooms to aid combustion.

The air in the four main boiler rooms was kept at higher than normal atmospheric pressure by means of these fans, and each room had to be entered through an air lock. The pressure was not very high, only about 5 inches of water gauge, though this was high enough to make your ears pop as you went through the lock. The theory behind this slightly higher pressure was delightfully simple, for of course the air in the boiler rooms, being at higher than atmospheric pressure, was always trying to escape, and the only way it could get out was through the oil burners, and this improved combustion considerably.

All the pumps mentioned above were of course electrically driven and this meant generating our own electricity on a fairly big scale. The ship had two power stations, the larger of these exclusively supplying power to the Engine Rooms, the other, which was only slightly smaller, feeding what was called the Hotel Services, that is, all the heating, lighting, cooking, ventilating, etc., indeed everything except the main propulsion of the vessel. This power station was fed from a separate boiler room which supplied steam at a slightly lower pressure and temperature. Each power plant was completely independent of the other, but in port when the electrical demand dropped considerably they could be linked together so that the Hotel Services Switchboard supplied the whole ship.

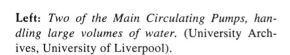

In all there were about 520 electric motors in the ship ranging in size from 5 HP up to 300 HP, and around 30,000 electric lamps. The galleys, capable of feeding a ship's company of over 3000, were all electric too, and there were 21 lifts or elevators. Apart from the steam that provided her propulsion she was virtually an all electric ship, and the publicity boys were quick to announce that her electrical generating plant was big enough to supply a town of 100,000 inhabitants.

Now all of this has gone. Originally there were five boiler rooms, two generating stations and two engine rooms, but apart from a section of the After Engine Room all this has gone, ripped out and discarded as being of no interest. To get it out must have cost the earth, and been almost as difficult as the installation, as to do so necessitated removal of many of the watertight bulkheads which are the very structure of the ship.

What is so regrettable is that all this equipment and machinery, though old and worn, was the last of its kind, the last example of the magnificent marine engineering skills of the 1930's. This machinery had served the *Queen Mary* well over a long and active life in which she had carried her passengers and crew in safety over millions of miles. Had it been still here today it would have been a money earner for the management, for there has been a great resurgence of interest in the ship as she originally was, and to have been able to walk through the boiler rooms, generating stations, and engine rooms would have been a major tourist attraction.

Left: *Two of the Main Circulating Pumps, handling large volumes of water.* (University Archives, University of Liverpool).

Chapter 3

Getting There Was Half the Fun

There is an old saying that there is no point in crying over spilt milk, nor can any useful purpose be served in the present instance by pointing a finger at whoever spilt it. Indeed it may be regarded as controversial that it was in fact a wrong decision to take out all the *Queen Mary*'s machinery in order to create large open spaces in which other activities could be carried on. It is quite true that her boilers and engines, and possibly also her electrical generating equipment, would never be required again, and from that point of view it might seem logical to sell it for what it would fetch. And also an assessment of the tourist market at that time did not warrant its retention.

To an outside observer in the 1990's, over 26 years after the *Queen Mary* came to Long Beach, it would seem that in those days the operators of the ship were not in the least interested in her as a ship, but rather as an interesting and unusually shaped building in which to do their own particular thing. In other words her principal attraction was the world wide publicity that she brought with her and the curiosity value she was bound to have. At that time it was possibly not seen that as the years went by the value of her machinery as an example of the best in British marine engineering was bound to increase. And no crystal ball could have predicted that the *Queen Mary* would be the lone survivor of the age of luxury liners.

One thing that was known in 1967 however er was that crossing the North Atlantic by sea was rapidly on its way out. The writing had been on the wall for some time. The Cunard dream of a two-ship regular weekly service actually came true in 1947 when, after years of frustration and disruption due

As Fougasse, famous 1930's cartoonist, saw it.

1st day   2nd day   3rd day   4th day

Above: *In Her home berth, The Ocean Dock, Southampton* (David F. Hutchings).

Below: *Heading down Southampton Water on another voyage.* (University Archives, University of Liverpool).

to the war, the *Queen Mary* and *Queen Elizabeth* finally were able to join forces and establish this service, and for over ten years they really had it all their own way, sailing from Southampton on Thursdays and from New York on Wednesdays. In that time Cunard White Star earned a small fortune.

But the fruitful period of high profits came to a pretty sudden end. The 1939-1945 war had seen a tremendous surge in the development of long range aircraft - unfortunately it takes a war to make dramatic increases in technology - and the establishment of the jet engine as a reliable and economic power unit came as the culmination. Quoted statistics, though varying slightly according to their source, tell the story plainly enough. In the mid 1950's Cunard were said to be carrying over 30% of all passengers crossing the Atlantic, and doing very nicely thank you. The airlines were still struggling to establish themselves, but by 1957 as many people crossed by air as by sea. In 1958 the first regular jet service was inaugurated, and only a year later the airlines were claiming

to have captured 63% of the market. In 1960 it has been stated that aircraft made 70,000 Atlantic crossings, and in 1961 the two Queens went into the red for the first time.

Not only the Queens faced a gloomy future, for the amount of sea going passenger traffic was in decline all over the world,

Far Right: *The Observation Bar as it was in 1936.* (University Archives, University of Liverpool).

Right: *Decor detail from a Main Deck Stateroom.* (University Archives, University of Liverpool).

Bottom Right: *A little comfort on your way across the Atlantic.* (University Archives, University of Liverpool).

Below: *The two starboard engine telegraphs on the navigating bridge.* (University Archives, University of Liverpool).

and the Port of Southampton, England's busiest passenger port, from which you could take a ship to any part of the world, also had to face up to the reality of the situation. The market continued to shrink, and the millions of passengers per annum which the Port handled in its heyday continued rapidly to dwindle. By 1974 the Port is said to have been handling only 350,000 per annum, and by 1982 this figure had dropped to under 75,000. Well may Cunard White Star have exchanged their slogan from "The only way to cross" to "Getting There is Half the Fun" in a desperate attempt to persuade travellers that a sea crossing had something extra to offer.

But nothing would stem the tide of progress, and early in 1967 Cunard regretfully announced that the *Queen Mary* would be withdrawn from service in September, and that the *Queen Elizabeth* would follow her in October 1968. This must have been a heart-breaking decision to take, but one look at the 'bottom line' of the trading account

was convincing proof that it was the only possible one. Both ships were put on the market, and many were the suggestions put forward for their future, perhaps the majority of them being highly impractical from an economic point of view.

Among the ideas that proliferated at this time were suggestions that the *Queen Mary* should be used as housing for the elderly or homeless, or become a top flight casino, or a mobile showroom for exports from Britain to the United States. There was also talk that an Australian syndicate would take her over and run her as an immigrant ship between Southampton and Sydney, or that an American syndicate would install her in New York as a tourist attraction and ultimately a school. Another suggestion was that she should become a floating hotel in Gibraltar. Some Philistines even mooted that she should simply be scrapped.

Perhaps it is hindsight that suggests now that the thought of keeping her in Britain as a monument to British marine engineering

A welcome from New York. (University of Liverpool).

Pier 90, the Queen Mary's New York Berth. (University Archives, University of Liverpool).

and initiative should have been pursued with more enthusiasm and diligence A home could, and perhaps should, have been found for her either in Southampton, her home port, or Liverpool, her port of registry, or in Glasgow, her birthplace, but we were not to know then that she was the last of her line and that we should never see her like again. All we could see was the horrendous cost of upkeep, and we did not have the vision to see what could be made of her.

Only the City of Long Beach had that vision, and believed that they could do something with her. A bargain was struck at $3.45 million, and following her 1001st Atlantic crossing she set out on the long haul to Long Beach and a retirement in the Californian sunshine. Ten thousand people are said to have watched her leave Southampton for the last time at the end of her career as an ocean liner.

At first sight this might be regarded as a good send-off, but compare it to the estimated two million who turned out to see her leave Clydebank at the beginning of her life. Perhaps this reduction in numbers is symbolic, and signifies that the public were no

longer sufficiently interested in her to wish to keep her. Maybe we were still suffering from war weariness and the subsequent apathy that comes from the realisation that our political lords and masters are seemingly quite incapable of keeping peace in the world.

Or maybe the media had not kept us sufficiently informed as to the details of her illustrious career, and it needed a gap of another 27 years - and a plethora of books on the subject - to help us realise that the *Queen Mary* was indeed something special, an astonishing achievement in the world of marine engineering, a shining monument to man's industry and vision that should be preserved at all costs. God Bless America for opening our eyes to this fact, and for providing her with a home.

Chapter 4

Personal Memories of a Great Ship

When the R.M.S. *Queen Mary* first steamed into Southampton, her home port, there was an air of excitement and expectancy in the town. She was not only the greatest ship the world had ever seen, but she had been built during a slump from which Britain was only slowly recovering, and she was regarded very much as a symbol of this recovery. The newspapers were full of information about her, so that it was natural that everyone in Southampton wanted to see her and, if possible, get aboard.

Friends have told me about the excitement of this day as they waited for the ship to arrive, for I was not with them at the time. I was already privileged to be aboard the *Queen Mary*, for I was a member of her crew. As we steamed up Southampton Water there was also a certain amount of excitement amongst the crew, for most of them were local men, and to them this was a home-coming, for they had been working aboard her in Clydebank during the last period of her fitting out.

As a young and recently qualified Electrical Engineer I was proud to be amongst her crew, having joined the ship three months previously in January 1936. With no previous sea-going experience I had written to Cunard offering my services, and was surprised and delighted when they accepted me. The three months on Clydeside were like a blissful dream, for I found myself in a strange and exciting new world. I had been on steamships before as a passenger, even on Clyde steamers that toured the lochs and the Western Isles, but had never experienced, or even imagined, anything like this bewilderingly enormous ocean liner.

For the first two weeks, together with another young man, John Rennie, who had joined on the same day, I walked for miles around the ship, tracing the electrical power distribution system with its two generating stations and fifty-two sub-stations. In the evenings we compared notes, discussed, and argued about, the quickest way to get from one part of the ship to another, and gradually familiarised ourselves with this monster of a ship that was to be our home for the next few years. It was all very strange and exciting.

Our three months stay in Clydebank passed very quickly and pleasantly. We were found lodgings by Cunard with Mr. Wylie, who was a Foreman Electrician in John Brown's Yard, and we could not have been more comfortable. Mr. Wylie and his family received us into their home and were hospitality itself, so that day followed day with bewildering speed.

During the last few months of the stay in the shipyard the pace of work became frantic - there was so much to do, and seemingly so little time. A host of carpenters, joiners, and other workmen were putting the finishing touches to passenger cabins, interior decorating specialists were completing their work, artists were fussing around making sure that their own individual contributions were in position and being displayed to the best advantage. Down below in the brightly lit engine rooms, boiler rooms, and generating stations, white overalled engineers were checking and rechecking every minutest details of the machinery which in a very

Leaving the Fitting Out Basin, 24 March 1936, watched by thousands of onlookers. (University Archives, University of Liverpool).

Two Tugs pull her head off the mud. (University Archives, University of Liverpool).

short space of time would spring into life and be vital for her safety and success.

At last the day arrived, all the thousands of items of stores were aboard, and gradually the many umbilical cords which had connected her to her mother for so many years were severed one by one. One of the most significant moments - perhaps more so to the engineers than to anyone else - was when the ship's own turbo-generators hummed into life and for the first time she was producing her own electricity, the life blood that from now on would sustain her wherever she should chance to go. The shore cables that had supplied her electricity hitherto were disconnected and dragged ashore, and at last she was no longer an appendage of the shipyard, but the R.M.S. *Queen Mary*, self contained, complete, and ready in all respects for sea.

When, during the morning of March 24th, her moorings were cast off and she began to move, very slowly, out into the river, a great cheer went up from the countless thousands who had assembled, on both banks of the river, to wish her God speed. There were many moist eyes at this moment, for she left,

At Full Speed off the Isle of Arran. In this trial she logged 32.84 knots, which at the time was a record. (David F. Hutchings).

not only a great hole in the landscape, a hole she had filled for years, but also she left a hole in the hearts of thousands of Clydesiders to whom, through many dark days and difficult times, she had represented life and security. With her went their good wishes and the proud knowledge that they had done their best to make her the greatest ship in the world. More than any other ship they had built she was "the pride of Clydebank".

There was excitement too when we left John Brown's shipyard and were towed down the Clyde to the sea, for half way down the river she went aground, and for a few minutes disaster threatened. On the notorious Dumbarton bend in the river her bow touched the mud, and before the tugs could pull her clear her stern was caught by the tide and went on the mud on the opposite bank. I was on deck at the time and for a few agonising moments wondered what on earth was going to happen next, but the pilot in charge remained icily calm and very quickly got her off and on her way downstream again.

The trials, most of which were held off the Isle of Arran, were fascinating but uneventful, perhaps the most interesting being a 24 hour full speed fuel consumption trial. At over 30 knots a ship can travel a long way in 24 hours, and we careered up and down the Irish Sea from Scotland to Lands End. As in the engine room most of us did not know where we were going it was always intriguing to come up off watch and find out where we were. At one point we saw the Mountains of Mourne in the distance, and at another the top of Blackpool Tower like a matchstick on the horizon.

Later, we carried out a two-day Channel cruise on which our passengers were Members of Parliament and other V.I.P's. The weather was not too good and I think many of our guests wished they had stayed at home. Some of the Cabin Stewards were not too pleased either, one told me that the tip he received from a prominent Labour politician was derisory. As we were returning from this cruise we passed the German liner *Bremen,* this being the first time we had met one of our principal competitors. The *Bremen* actually treated us with great courtesy, her band was on deck playing God Save the King as we passed, and she flew a six flag hoist in greeting. I happened to be on the bridge at the time and was amazed at

Main Switchboard, Machinery Services. (University Archives, University of Liverpool).

the reaction to this friendly gesture. No one had expected it and there was a rush, first to read the *Bremen's* message, for the flags were almost end on to us and we were both travelling at speed and rapidly drawing apart, and then to concoct a suitable reply. This was the first time the flag locker had been used, and some of the flags were in the wrong pigeon holes, so that ultimately they all had to come out and the bridge was literally ankle deep in flags. A message was finally put together and flown, but alas the *Bremen* by this time was almost out of sight.

The weeks of April and May passed very quickly and pleasantly as the ship was gradually made ready for the Maiden Voyage. John Rennie and I shared digs in Southampton in Morris Rod, the Polygon, at the home of a Miss Miller, a motherly soul who was also a very good cook. We had nothing to complain about and every day was full of interest. As the only two electrical engineers with no home ties in Southampton we willingly took on jointly the task of manning the switchboard on the ship at night, for we had one turbo-generator running continuously to supply the ship's electrical requirements. We went on duty at 5 p.m. and were there until relieved at 8 a.m. the following morning. There was very little to do and, as only one of us needed to be down below at a time it was possible for us both to get a little sleep.

This left the daytime free, and we were able to do a considerable amount of exploring. Neither of us knew the area, and we were delighted to discover the New Forest and of course the Isle of Wight. To me at this time life still had a dream-like quality and I could hardly believe that it was real. The difference between the life I was now leading, not only working on this fabulous ship but with time to explore the beautiful countryside around Southampton, and my previous work in a dark and dreary factory in the heart of the Black Country was so marked as to be almost unbelievable.

The day of the Maiden Voyage, 27th May 1936, dawned bright and clear, and excitement reached its climax as the passengers came aboard. Every berth had been booked for months, and I have never seen such an excited bunch of people. Passengers and the friends who were seeing them off hurried about the ship, trying to see as much as possible, continually being charmed and astonished at what they found. Though the media had for a long time been flooding the world with descriptions of the ship's decor and furnishings, no one seeing her for the first time had expected anything like the magnificence and opulence of the accommodation that she was providing for her passengers.

The pitch and volume of excitement was such that it seemed almost impossible that the atmosphere would ever return to normal, but return it did in due course, the visitors

and friends were all shepherded ashore, gangways bearing the proud legend R.M.S. *Queen Mary* were withdrawn, moorings were singled up and then cast off, and with one long blast from her deep throated whistle we were away, saying good-bye to Southampton and the thousands of cheering people who had crammed every vantage point to see us leave. The *Queen Mary*'s career had really begun.

When we reached New York the reception we received was tumultuous. Long before we sighted land we were met by three aircraft who circled around and escorted us in. At the mouth of the Hudson River a veritable armada of boats was there to welcome us, hundreds of them, of every conceivable type and size. They were all crammed to the gunwales with sightseers, and all had their whistles or horns in continuous song, the noise and general confusion being indescribable. Even after we were docked, alongside our specially prepared berth on Pier 90, a seemingly endless procession of boats came as close as they could, to have a look.

The following day the ship was thrown open to the public, and New Yorkers in their thousands flocked aboard, the interest they took in every single detail being staggering. The Chief Steward's Department had laid up the main dining room for dinner, so that our visitors could see the style in which passengers lived, and it certainly looked splendid with its brand new cutlery, crockery, glass, and menu cards, but alas they had reckoned without souvenir hunters who gradually stripped the room of everything moveable. By the end of the day the room was bare.

New York to me was a strange and somewhat disturbing place. The pace of life was faster than I was used to, and the city was full of strange sights and smells. The morning papers came out at 9.30 p.m. the previous evening, and were not only published in several sections, but also apparently in other languages besides English. It was common

The fantastic New York welcome on the Maiden Voyage, 1 June 1936. (University Archives, University of Liverpool).

practice for people to buy a paper from one of the many news stands on Broadway and discard the bits they did not want, and late in the evening the streets were littered with newspapers blowing about. The sidewalks were generally filthy and covered with trodden-in chewing gum, some of which stuck to the soles of your shoes. Broadway, particularly in the vicinity of Times Square, did not come to life until nearly midnight and was still thronged at 2 a.m., by which time all good sailors should have been back on their ship!

After we had recovered from the excitement of the maiden voyage, and another, though more restrained reception back in Southampton, we settled down to the routine of regular weekly crossings. Every other Wednesday morning we left Southampton for Cherbourg and New York, and on the alternate Wednesdays we left New York for home. It was a relentless schedule for in the early days we had teething troubles with some of the plant which necessitated extra hours of work, and there were trips in bad weather when we were forced to slow down and were consequently late in getting in - but we still had to be off again on Wednesday morning. I can well remember one period in the winter of 1936 when the weather was particularly bad - we were told later that it was the worst in living memory - when for two consecutive voyages, due to extra work that had to be fitted in, I hardly saw daylight for a month, and never even got off the ship in the few hours we were in Southampton turning round.

This was of course exceptional, though few people in 9 a.m. to 5 p.m. jobs realise the hours that sailors could be called upon to work in those days. Maybe it is easier today, but at that time the basic week at sea was of 56 hours - seven days at eight hours a day. There were no weekend breaks, no Bank Holidays, Good Friday or Christmas Day. If the ship was at sea there was no argument, you had to work. Most of the Engineers worked normal sea watches, that is to say, four hours on duty followed by eight hours off, the 12 hour clock being divided into three watches - 8 to 12, 12 to 4 and 4 to 8.

In addition there were "Stand-By" watches when the ship was leaving or entering port, or steaming in fog, and these could jump up your hours considerably. On "Stand-By" the watch down below was doubled up, which meant that in the worst case instead of working four hours with eight hours off you could be down below for eight hours with only four hours off. In the *Queen Mary* there were many "Stand-By" watches for she was frequently leaving or arriving at Southampton, Cherbourg or New York, and there was plenty of fog in the North Atlantic.

Every voyage too we changed watches, the net result of this being a complete disruption

One of the 52 Auxiliary Switchboards throughout the ship. (University Archives, University of Liverpool).

of sleep patterns, your body never being able to settle down into a routine that lasted more than a couple of weeks. On top of this, and by far the most disruptive force was the daily time change. New York time is five hours behind European time, so that on our eastwards crossing the ship's clocks were put forward one hour each night at eleven o'clock. So that on the first night out when the clocks said it was eleven o'clock your body was saying that really it was only ten. On the second night out at eleven o'clock ships time your body thought it was nine o'clock, on the third night out eight o'clock, the fourth night seven o'clock, and on the night we reached Europe six o'clock, by which time your body was so utterly confused as to find sleep impossible.

With all these drawbacks then, how is it that men ever go to sea, and what is more, stay there? This puzzled me when I first became a sailor, but I soon realised there is a strange and subtle relationship between you and your ship. You become very attached to her. She is not only your workplace and your home; you also depend on her for your very existence. And above all she is feminine; she is both your mother and your mistress, loving, kind, unpredictable, infuriating, but loveable. She is feminine - no sailor ever refers to his ship as "it", always "she".

This realisation came as a great shock to me one voyage in that first winter of 1936, and I would like to quote a couple of paragraphs from my book "*Queen Mary*: Her Early Years Recalled".

"One winter's day in Southampton when the ship was due to sail I caught my tram as usual in the early morning to go down to the docks. It was dark, cold, pouring with rain, and I was miserable. I had recently been married and we were very comfortable in our flat in the Polygon. I did not want to leave my warm and cosy home to be tossed about on that wretched Atlantic. We were short of money, and I had put off paying the electricity bill to the point that I was now worried that they might come and turn it off. My shoes needed repairing and I had stepped into a puddle with the one that was leaking. The tram was full of silent, wet, rather objectionable bodies, and it jolted to and fro in a disgusting way.

In short, I was full of all the normal petty irritations and worries which are associated with life on land. Two days later we were

Diane Rush.

RON WINTER AND MARY . . . . . . SHE THEN PUT HER NOSE DOWN — JUST TO SHOW YOU

well out into the Atlantic, heading into a moderately rough sea, and I was on deck, leaning on the rail, smoking my pipe, and gazing at the water. I tried to remember all the troubles that had beset me when I left home, and though I could remember what they were, I was completely unable to stir up any emotion about any of them. They had all retreated into the background, and had no more substance or reality than last night's bad dream. I was shocked to find that I did not have a care in the world. My pipe was drawing evenly, the sea stretched away to the horizon on all sides, and I was at peace."

And that is really what it is all about. Your ship rules your life, and the *Queen Mary* certainly ruled mine. This does not mean that you stop loving your wife, or do not get homesick. Far from it; sometimes you get a great longing for home comforts and a shore life, and sometimes this wins. But I shall never forget the feeling of desolation, almost panic, when I left the ship for good and saw her sail away without me. After

crossing the Atlantic 94 times in her, in good weather and in bad, she was more than just a ship to me.

The *Queen Mary* is a long way away now, in Long Beach, California, where she is a 400 room hotel and conference centre. She is a considerable tourist attraction, and has gained the affection of the many who work aboard her. Happily I have not lost touch, and have made many friends among those who now serve her, some of whom have visited me in England. Public tours of the ship are popular, and I am happy that my taped voice is used as part of the commentary, and here at home I am privileged to give talks and slide shows about life aboard her in those first three glorious years.

But what a pity she was ever sold out of this country! She should by rights be docked now in Southampton, her home port, or in Glasgow, her birthplace. Here she would be a major tourist attraction, and a perpetual reminder of Britain's once maritime greatness.

Chapter 5

The Anatomy of a Ship

This is a chapter of gripes. A chronicle of all the changes made in the ship since her early days which I find baffling, disappointing, and in some cases downright deplorable. Some of these criticisms may be unjustified but they are based on information that has come to me from various sources over the past 25 years, and on my own observations when visiting the ship on the occasion of the 'glorious 59th' anniversary in September 1993. I promise I will try and make this the last bit of negative writing in the book, for we must now look forward - which I am sure we are all doing - and plan positively for the future which, from where I am sitting in England shows some signs of being both encouraging and exciting. But first, let me get one or two things off my chest.

I will spare you any further gripes about the problems down below, apart from stressing the deplorable removal of so many of her watertight bulkheads, for this struck a blow at the very strength and nature of the vessel herself. To anyone who loves ships this is akin to vandalism. Thankfully though, I am told by an expert that there would be no major problem in replacing them, except of course the common disadvantage associated with most restoration work of having to take the ship out of service while it is carried out. But the question of the bulkheads brings me to what I believe is a basic principle concerning the anatomy of the ship. I refer to the Working Alleyway.

Not being an expert in ship design I cannot say whether this principle applies to all passenger ships, although I believe it does, but in the *Queen Mary* I do know that the life and smooth operation of this very complex ship did revolve around the Working Alleyway. In the *Queen Mary* at sea the Working Alleyway on D Deck was the backbone of the ship, it ran almost from one end of the vessel to the other, and it is impossible to over-emphasise its importance. It was the spinal column, the main artery, the nerve centre, call it what you will, but every function of the ship except steering her stemmed from the Working Alleyway.

Is this an over-simplification of the situation I wonder? Maybe it is an Engineer's eye view, but from the Working Alleyway you got a clearer perspective of the responsibilities and work of other departments. The deck officers and their department were responsible for taking the vessel from A to B in safety and to a schedule. The pursers, stewards and catering staff were responsible for the well being of the passengers and crew, all vital parts of the organisation. From his eyrie like bridge seven decks higher up, the Captain, who carried the ultimate and fearsome responsibility for the whole outfit, was entirely dependent on the Working Alleyway for his control of the ship, though I don't think he visited it very often. I certainly never saw him there, but then as a junior officer I was separated from him in rank by 80 other engineer officers, headed by a Chief Engineer and a Staff Chief Engineer, both of whom were themselves fairly remote beings who seldom impinged visibly on our working lives.

But this is a digression from a consideration of the importance of this part of the ship. From the Working Alleyway you could readily reach any of the boiler rooms, generating stations, or engine rooms which were immediately below, or the galleys, dining rooms, and passenger accommodation which were immediately above, while all around you on D Deck were the storerooms, offices and administration of this huge complex. As its name was meant to imply the Working Alleyway was a very busy main thoroughfare.

It was the connecting link between all these various functions, so that it is not difficult to appreciate that if it is removed, abolished, done away with, the cohesion of the remainder is bound to suffer, for there is nothing left to tie the various parts together. What would happen to a small town if you took away its Main Street? Or to a human body of you removed its spine? And this appears to have been exactly what was done to the *Queen Mary*, possibly in her early days in Long Beach, and presumably because it was believed that the Working Alleyway was now redundant and in the way.

So large stretches of it were removed, and it would seem that the result was confusion in place of cohesion. This would explain why so many of the early alterations carried out appear to have been haphazard and uncoordinated. Obviously there was a broad plan, and it must be admitted that most of the alterations were efficiently carried out with a high standard of workmanship, but the overall impression is of piecemeal development and the destruction of many worthwhile features in the ship.

Another example may illustrate the point, and this one concerns the Promenade Deck. The first class section of the Promenade Deck was originally one of the wonders of the ship. "Three times round to the mile!" was the proud boast, though I see this was subsequently modified to four times round to the mile. But never mind, the point is that it was once possible to walk right round, and this fact produced much good publicity. You can no longer do this, on account of the Observation Lounge extension, the Chelsea

One of the few remaining bits of the Working Alleyway, not truly representative of what it was like.

Restaurant, and the Promenade Café, and excellent as these establishments are they are insufficient compensation. Is it an impossible dream to hope that one day the Promenade Deck will be restored to its pristine magnificence? In a later chapter I shall return to this subject and put forward a few suggestions.

While still on the Promenade Deck perhaps it is permissible to express regret at the deterioration of the teak laid decking itself. This was once another of the glories of the ship and it is now in a sorry state. One has to

Port side of the Promenade Deck in 1936. Magnificent! (University Archives, University of Liverpool).

remember of course that the old lady is nearly 60 years old and that many thousands of feet have trodden her decks, but teak is a marvellous and long wearing wood if properly treated, and for a start it should never be varnished but only oiled.

Wear and tear is of course inevitable, and when critically assessing the *Queen Mary* today it is important not to forget that there have been four quite distinct phases in her life.

Top Right: *Souvenir of the Long Gallery. The "Green Cow"*. (University Archives, University of Liverpool).
Bottom Right: *Souvenir of the Long Gallery. "Evening on the Avon"*. (University Archives, University of Liverpool).

1. 1936-1939. The first three truly glorious years when she was indeed a wonder ship. Everything about her was spanking new, she was replete with specially created furnishing fabrics, carpets, furniture, crockery, cutlery, linen, etc. etc., not to mention the paintings, murals, sculptures and other artistic decorations contributed by Britain's best artists. Alas, this was not to last and it was rudely terminated by the war.

2. 1939-1947. Much of her finery was stripped out as she was converted in stages for troop carrying, until ultimately she could carry a ship's company of nearly 16,000, an incredible number to be accommodated in one ship. Conditions for her many passengers were almost unbearable, and it was amazing that more damage to her fabric did not occur.

3. 1947-1967. Conversion back to luxury liner status was not easy in a world impoverished by seven years of war, and with the best will in the world her new decor could not be expected to match her pre-war splendour. Some of her art treasures never did return to the ship.

4. 1967 Long Beach. After 31 years of extremely active life it must have been a comfort for her to find a safe haven in the Californian sunshine, and one can well believe that much work needed to be done to fit her for her new role.

All these four phases were entirely different, and the last three have each necessitated violent changes, but at least she herself has survived, unlike the majority of her competitors, and perhaps we should be surprised, not at the damage that has been done, but that so much of her original decor remains. Enough and plenty, anyway, to make restoration possible and worthwhile.

Among the disappointments that have to be registered is the down market movement of the Observation Lounge and the Verandah

Above: *Part of the Doris Zinkeisen Mural, once in the Verandah Grill. Now down below.* (University Archives, University of Liverpool).

Right: *Tourist Class Swimming Pool. Alas, no more.*

Bottom Right, and far right : *Illuminated Glass Panel in Swimming Pool Entrance.*

Grill. These two were the most elegant and sophisticated rooms in the ship, and though the Observation Lounge has not slipped very far, the Verandah Grill has really plunged. It seems incomprehensible to have turned the Verandah Grill into, of all things, a Burger Bar, and then to have built a sophisticated restaurant, Sir Winston's, on top of it. And what a strange home was found for the Doris Zinkeisen mural! Hers must be one of the ghosts that are reputed to haunt the ship.

Other disappointments include the disappearance of the Long Gallery, the Starboard Gallery, the Ballroom, and various other rooms, and the Second Class Swimming Pool. It is also disappointing that the beautiful First Class Swimming Pool has never been put to use, and that indeed the after deck was completely vandalised and cleared with a view to installing an outside pool. The Starboard Gallery did of course disap-

pear as such in 1947 when it was turned into a cinema for first and second class passengers, the provision of a cinema being an improvement on the original practice of showing films in the Main Lounge.

The Long Gallery was originally a very restful room, its ambience being enhanced by the two large pictures, one at each end. The after one, a beautiful painting by Algernon Newton called "Evening on the Avon" is now tucked away in what is, I believe, the Board Room, while the forward one, "A Sussex Landscape" by Bertram Nicholls has suffered an even more curious fate. This painting, as of September 1993, is now behind the counter in "Ye Olde Fudge Factory and Juice Bar". Happily the picture, which was affectionately known to certain members of the crew as "The Green Cow", is now hidden by a giant poster, otherwise questions might be asked as to what types of juice are on sale here. Perhaps milk is one of them. A third part of the Long Gallery now provides an attractive entrance to the Chelsea Restaurant, and it must be said that the decor of this entrance is superb, as is the seafood served in the restaurant itself.

So perhaps this chapter is not all gripes

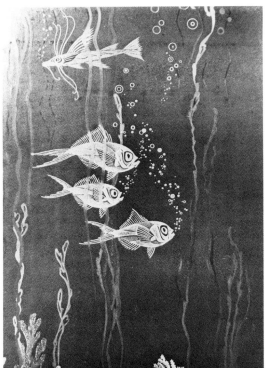

Above: *Detail of the fabulous decor in the children's room.* (University Archives, University of Liverpool).

Below: *A proud and beautiful ship if ever there was one.* (University Archives, University of Liverpool).

after all, for the alterations that have been made, though many are regrettable, have been carried out to a very high standard, and the parts of the ship now seen by the public are mainly very presentable, and a credit to those who created them and to those who look after them.

In the present climate of positive thinking, and the desire to return, wherever possible to original standards, the future appears to be promising and even exciting. It is of course impossible completely to turn the clock back and recreate the ambience of 1936. Too much has been lost and can never be reproduced. Also of course our tastes and fashions have changed over the years, and many things we regarded as first class in 1936 can now appear to be very old fashioned and even dowdy. But it would be a mistake to believe that people today are not interested in the old fashioned styles of 1936, and I would like to quote an instance in support of this. Osborne House, in the Isle of Wight in England, was the home of Queen Victoria - another Queen - and she died there in 1901. The Royal Apartments, including her bedroom and the room in which she and the Prince Consort worked, have been preserved exactly as they were on the day she died, and the hundreds of thousands of visitors who find their way to the Isle of Wight just to see these rooms is proof that the past has a great fascination for many people.

And whatever the fashions of the day may be, the *Queen Mary* has already proved that she has a strange fascination for many people, and that her own individual and extraordinary character has still much to offer. Long may she live to excite admiration and wonder, not only in this century but in the next.

Chapter 6

The Queen Mary in Long Beach
by Diane Rush

On December 9th, 1967, the *Queen Mary* glided through the ingress to Long Beach Harbor, prophetically named many years before, "Queen's Gate". This coincidence was by no means the only one to suggest the *Queen Mary*'s destiny was as carefully designed as the ship herself.

If a single word could be used to describe the recurrent pattern woven into the fabric of the R.M.S. *Queen Mary*'s tapestry, it is renaissance. The Great Depression threatened job #534 with abandonment. With the merging of the White Star and Cunard shipping lines and with a government loan, the desolate frame of the unnamed ship was completed, soon to prove herself as the epitome of maritime excellence. 31 years later, faced with retirement from service as a transatlantic liner, the *Queen Mary* overcame impossible odds for a second time. Demonstrating versatility, she became a popular hotel, museum and convention hall for Long Beach as well as a landmark for this industrial seaport. Precariously balanced on the whims of fate once again in 1992, it seemed her sale to foreign interests was imminent. Port Commission and City Council meetings were regularly attended by employees of the ship and by historic preservationists who registered their support for keeping the *Queen Mary* in Long Beach and appointing an administrator to finance and operate the

attraction. The 'Daughter of the Clyde' had become too much a part of the soul of Long Beach to relinquish.

In the 26 years that the *Queen Mary* has graced the Long Beach skyline, the American psyche has been imbued with her presence. One of the most eloquent expressions to this effect was communicated by the artistry of a sand-sculpture contestant on a Southern California beach. His work depicted the continental United States bordered on the east coast by an outsized Statue of Liberty and on the west, a *Queen Mary* the length of his map's California. It was pleasing to be reminded that America was watched over by these two great ladies.

What was the genesis of this bond between Long Beach and the *Queen Mary*? For decades Long Beach had been a shipbuilding and industrial city, endowed with offshore oil, geographic features conducive to a seaport and mild climate. In spite of productivity, commerce and natural resources, the miles of refineries, brick buildings and dockyards imparted a sense of impermanence and loneliness. Long Beach was a transfer point, a temporary container for people, goods and vessels bound for some other destination. The *Queen Mary*, by contrast, was the essence of stability and culture. Yet, for all the traditions of quality and service the *Queen Mary* represented, the world she was designed to

The start of her last voyage. (University Archives, University of Liverpool).

compete in was rapidly vanishing. The ship's survival would depend upon a major center of commerce with a built-in tourist population willing to invest in her potential as an attraction. Not only did Long Beach have the space and pecuniary means required but the need to claim something of great sentimental worth as uniquely her own.

Since 1958 Long Beach City planners had been developing a scheme to highlight the waterfront with a museum of the sea. During the following decade, business expanded tremendously in the Long Beach area creating a demand for new hotels. The nearby communities of Buena Park and Anaheim flourished in the 1960's, their reputations established by Knott's Berry Farm and Disneyland, respectively. Long Beach was

searching for something big with a maritime theme that could answer the competition. The 1,019 ft. Cunarder fitted every specification! Other advantages were the proximity of the Long Beach Naval Shipyard which had the only dry-dock in Southern California that could accommodate the massive vessel and the temperate seasons of the California coast which promised easy maintenance to her hull and superstructure.

Cunard was flooded with bids for the sister Queens and even after eliminating such offers as the one from a man in Little Rock, Arkansas, who envisioned the two ships welded together to form the world's largest catamaran, there were still 18 viable contenders. Long Beach placed the highest bid, but only by a 50,000 dollar margin over a

Safely berthed, and dominating her surroundings.

company from Pennsylvania. 3.45 million dollars for the historic steamship proved to be the bargain of the century. The scrap value alone was set at the figure of 2 million dollars. In addition, the City of Long Beach was in the advanced stages of negotiations with the California Museum Foundation to construct an 8. million dollar maritime museum. The ship could be used to house the displays instead, saving the Foundation expenses that could eventually go towards the upgrading of exhibits.

34 years after the restart of job #534 was announced in Clydebank, almost to the day, the mammoth liner was to begin a transformation far from the river of her birth. For a solid month shipyard workers removed 3 of the 4 manganese-bronze propellers, encasing the outboard port prop and bossing in a "viewing box" welded to her hull. The Denny Brown stabilisers were likewise removed and 320 tons of accumulated paint was sand-blasted from the rivet-studded cliffs of steel. Even the paint chips were turned to capital gain. Made into cuff-links and paperweights, the paint chips, filed at an angle, told a chronology of events in the ship's career with layers of paint. The first coat was the protective red lead layer covered with successive white layers broken only by one thin grey line indicating her war time coat.

The first of several obstacles presented itself after the City of Long Beach designated the *Queen Mary* as a "Class A Floating Building". This was presumably a measure to avoid the high taxes associated with a sea going vessel. A host of maritime unions protested, declaring that a ship was a ship and they were entitled to any and all work pertaining to the conversion. The controversy was exacerbated when the Mary went to the Naval Shipyard dry-dock. The civilian union workers felt this action was creating competition between the service and private industry. After the ensuring strikes and delays, it was determined by California state labour officials that the land-based unions had jurisdiction. The labor cost represented a 20% increase over the figure projected by Long Beach planners rendering any financial advantages of her 'floating building' status dubious.

Due to the highly specialised nature of the

An ocean liner and a lady.

Queen Mary's conversion, the City of Long Beach formed the *Queen Mary* Department to co-ordinate the project. The Museum of The Sea Foundation, a non-profit organisation working in conjunction with the *Queen Mary* Department, developed the Jacques Cousteau Living Sea Museum in what had been the forward engine room and boiler room #5.

Tragically, every piece of propulsion machinery from the forward engine room to auxiliary boiler room #1 has been removed save for a solitary Centrex ballast pump. The removal of the components of the *Queen Mary*'s powertrain was conducted by Lipsett and Co. between May 1968 and April 1969. Bulkheads separating the 4 main boiler rooms were cut away and all 24 Yarrow watertube boilers, 3 scotch boilers, the water softening plant, 7 turbo-generators, 2 sets of quadruple-expansion steam turbines and the two line shafts for the outboard props, condensers, circulating pumps and associated machinery were lifted up through the funnel hatches and sold for scrap or discarded.

With over 20,000 tons of propulsion machinery and structural members removed, the ship needed compensation for this weight. 46 of the 66 wing tanks were pumped full of a dense compound of Bentonite and limestone; drilling mud. This solved the ballast problem simultaneously protecting the steel from oxidation and acting as an anti-bacterial agent.

For 3 years the *Queen Mary* remained at pier E where she underwent drastic alterations. It has been reported that the ship's rusting funnels were held together only by 100 coats of paint and when removed, collapsed under their own weight. What this unchallenged statement neglected to mention was the fact these funnels were seared off with acetylene torches, hoisted via crane devoid of casings and dumped upon the dockside.

Maintenance of a ship the size of the *Queen Mary* presented a variety of demands. One consideration was electrolysis, especially where unlike metals were joined. The hull was fitted with a cathodic protection system to produce a slight electrical field to counteract electrolytic action. Sensors connected to rectifiers inside the ship could be regularly monitored to ascertain if the current was

A Queen high and dry. (David F. Hutchings).

sufficient. Marine divers would conduct physical surveys at 6 month intervals, replacing sacrificial zinc anodes when necessary.

The first master commercial lessee on board was Diner's Continental Corporation, known also as Diner's *Queen Mary*. This principal operator was named in March, 1968 and would be responsible for the development of restaurants, shops, hotel management and other commercial aspects of the ship. Specifications in the contract called for refitting of utility systems and structural modifications to decks and bulkheads. Unfortunately, the contract was breached on over 30 particular items causing an estimated 139 million dollars in damage. By July of 1970, Diners *Queen Mary* terminated their participation in the venture and it was almost a year later before another operator was installed.

In November of 1968, a public auction was held and countless objects from the *Queen Mary* were up for bid. Silverware, china, various fittings, doors and furniture from the tourist and third-class cabins were among the items available. These artefacts were regarded by the public as sacred and some went to extravagant lengths to secure possession of memorabilia.

The necessity of converting various utilities was daunting but with the additional task of correcting previous errors made in the refit, prospective lessees would count the cost of investing in this 'Pandora's Box'. Even a comparatively uncomplicated project involved the replacement of the 220 volt direct current wiring with American standard 110 volt alternating current electrical cable which included 4,000 miles of the material and over 30,000 fixtures! Updated fire alarm systems, fire sprinklers, plumbing modifications, air conditioning and heating improvements, implementation of a security alarm detection system and the restructuring of decks and bulkheads accounted for tremendous budget increases.

The original estimate of 8.75 million to make recommended improvements almost quadrupled before the ship opened to the public on May 8, 1971. Only one month prior, the new lessee, Speciality Restaurants Corporation, took over the operation. Though the museum and lower decks were still in transition and many shops and restaurants on the Promenade Deck had not opened for trade, 92% of the polled visitors claimed they would return. During the first months as a tourist attraction, the *Queen Mary* was open exclusively on weekends and the admission price for adults was a mere $2. 14,000 people swarmed the decks on Memorial Day (last Monday in May). By the end of 1971, Jacques Cousteau's Living Sea Museum was added to the growing list of amenities. Locals' curiosity was piqued by advertisements of this newly completed exhibit. Attendance reached a summit on February 20, 1972. 19,600 people had come to see the *Queen Mary* in a single day, a record that still stands at the time of this writing. The efforts and faith of the city had paid off. From May 1971 to August 1972, over 1,900,000 thrilled in discovery or quietly reminisced on board the greatest liner ever built.

An article published in the Los Angeles Times' West magazine in December 1970, observed that the *Queen Mary* was the agony and ecstasy of Long Beach. Entitled, *100 Million Lbs. of Trouble, But What a Woman!*, this report declared, "Long Beach now has come far enough with the *Queen Mary* to realise she is a very expensive lady indeed. But that was to be expected. And, she could be worth every cent when all is said and done. Of course, there still is quite a bit to be said and done."Spread across two pages is an accompanying photograph of the *Queen Mary*'s stem towering above the forms of workmen in the Long Beach Naval dry-dock. Viewing the picture gives a graphic and balanced perspective of the aesthetic joy and crushing responsibility experienced by the ship's providers.

Increasing traffic justified the integration of hotel accommodations with commercial attractions and tours. Pacific Southwest Airlines (PSA) took charge of the *Queen Mary*'s hotel, making the first 150 of 400 rooms available on November 2, 1972, 5 years after the ship first came to Long Beach. The PSA Hotel *Queen Mary* daily rates for 1971-1973 are listed as follows:

	Single	Double
Twin (Inside)	$22.00	$26.00
Twin (Port)	$24.00	$28.00
Twin (Starboard)	$26.00	$30.00
King (Inside)	$24.00	$28.00
King (Port)	$26.00	$30.00
King (Starboard)	$28.00	£32.00
Triples		
King with Single	$40.00	$50.00
King with Twins	$45.00	$55.00
One Bedroom Suite	$70.00	$90.00
Two Bedroom Suite	$100.00	$120.00

Each additional person in room....... $5.00
6% tax to all rate

"Passengers" had 4 restaurants, 4 cocktail lounges with nightly entertainment, International boutiques, a museum of oceanography, convention facilities and even a Bank of America. For the first time in history, ordinary citizens or tourists could enjoy the adventure and ambience normally reserved for the wealthy or for the working class after a lifetime of saving.

All of the original cabin-class and some expanded tourist-class cabins aft comprise the ship's hotel, occupying most of Main, A-Deck and B-Deck. Except for carpeting and miscellaneous vending machines in stairway landings, these upper decks appear much as they always have. Each deck and cabin has its own unique character. Adorned in 56 varieties of rare woods, the *Queen Mary*'s interiors exude gracious warmth. The patterns in avodire, quilted maple and English elm burr seem as deliberate and ornate as enamelled guilloche. According to H.T.W. Bousfield, author of *R.M.S. Queen Mary, The Ship of Beautiful Woods*, "The term 'veneer' must not be misunderstood. A veneer is sometimes ignorantly imagined to describe a sham. In fact, a proper veneer is a thin layer of wood that must be either too delicate to be strong in bulk or, indeed, too rare and rich to be used at all, unless spread on some worthy substance (after all, one has to spread caviar on toast). A strong, tough wooden base of no artistic distinction is

Above: *Inlay work from the 3rd Class Garden
Lounge. "The Ship of Beautiful Woods".*
Left: *Anna Zinkeisen painting in the Ballroom.*
Below Left: *Another painting by Anna Zinkeisen.*

therefore covered by a thin layer of exquisite
wood - as the pillars of the Temple of
Solomon were overlaid with fine gold...."

Polished wood veneers or marquetry panels provide a luxurious background for the
fittings and ornamentation of the suites and
staterooms on Main Deck. Most of these
contain multiple bedrooms, baths, sitting
parlors, wardrobes and even kitchenettes.
Original light fixtures, beveled, etched and
tinted mirrors as well as built-in desks, cabi-
nets and dressers amaze with their beauty
and novel application. Cabins on A and B
decks are smaller and less ornate but
nonetheless cosy and appealing.

On A-Deck an uninterrupted view of the
ship's length can be appreciated in either of
the two corridors of the hotel. The sheer of
the vessel is quite pronounced. When standing at either extreme end you can observe,
towards the center, the deck and rows of
doors sweep in a downward curve, while at
the opposite end, hundreds of feet distant,
you can see the rising continuation of that
arc. B-Deck is deeper in the ship, remarkable for its labyrinth of athwartship passages
and interesting alcoves formed by the inter-
ception of the Grand Salon's dome. The
Hotel Lobby and Starboard Lounge, formerly the cabin-class purser's office and doc-
tor's consulting room, are, like the entire
hotel area, highly photogenic. Most enduring
of all pictures is the memory of a view of
Long Beach Harbor in the moonlight from a
cabin aboard the *Queen Mary*.

Even in the early 1970's it was apparent
the *Queen Mary* needed experienced management and continuous development to
attract business. In March of 1974, the Hyatt
Corporation took control of the hotel facilities. This transfer coincided with the opening of a new complex of shops situated
alongside the ship. Mary's Gate Village, as it
was called, was a handsome 3/4 scale reproduction of an English town which reinforced
the British theme and enhanced the impres-

sion of the ship's wondrous size. Mary's Gate Village has been twice renamed, once London towne and presently, the Queen's Marketplace.

Like its predecessor, Pacific Southwest Airlines, Hyatt Corporation advertised the ample Cunarder as "81,000 tons of fun". The City of Long Beach had some officials who might well have hung the title, "Little Ship of Horrors" on her for her voracious demands. But, where much is given, much is expected. Motivated to find solutions for problems inherent in a project like the *Queen Mary*, Long Beach confronted and overcame a series of obstacles that vastly advanced the city as a commercial and cultural center. Financing and marketing the ship put Long Beach on the map. 30 years ago, if a person said they were from Long Beach, the image of oil wells and warehouses came to mind. Today, anywhere in the world, Long Beach means the *Queen Mary*.

From 1967 to 1977, the *Queen Mary* was owned by the City of Long Beach and leased to a series of operators during that period. Another option was considered, turning the vessel over to the Port of Long Beach since the Harbor Commission dealt more specifically with issues of shipping, the tidelands and properties on the shoreline. It seemed appropriate to consolidate the lessees under the jurisdiction of one operator. In 1978, the *Queen Mary* was officially signed over to the Port. Two years later, on September 1, 1980, the Wrather Corporation formed a subsidiary with the Port of Long Beach, Wrather Port Properties, Ltd., and agreed to a 66 year lease to manage the ship and adjoining acreage.

What structure fabricated by human hands has survived twice its life-expectancy and performed such a variety of functions? If the *Queen Mary* had to submit a résumé to prospective operators, the only two experiences missing would be flying and diving!

The *Queen Mary* may be the only landmark and monument expected to "earn her keep". The Long Beach press has been a notorious detractor of its city's most prosperous symbol. Appropriation of funds from the City of Long Beach through tideland oil revenue has been routinely misrepresented by the media and politicians seeking to blame operating costs of the ship for budget deficits. California, and particularly the Long Beach - San Pedro areas, are blessed with an almost inexhaustible supply of natural oil, on and off-shore. Long Beach has produced over half of the oil revenue for the state of California for years and is entitled to a percentage of the revenue to develop shoreline projects. As far back as the mid-

1950's, California allocated 250 million dollars to finance shoreline improvements specifying the then non-existent maritime museum! The tide-land funds are public monies which can be spent on improvements and developments used by the public such as streets, bridges, shopping malls or convention centers. Politicians have taken advantage of the connotation of public monies to imply taxpayer's dollars.

D. Christopher Davis, President of the Long Beach Area Convention and Visitor's Council, contested such attitudes with research statistics. Nearly 30% of all visitors to Long Beach polled in a 1991 survey, claimed the *Queen Mary* was their primary destination. According to Davis, any convention held in Long Beach had the potential for generating a million dollars from hotel, food and entertainment expenditures. The *Queen Mary*'s positive influence is both pervasive and intangible, making her value to the city difficult to chart. However, Davis asserted that in 1991, the ship generated 418.3 million dollars in direct and indirect revenue.

Three years after the Wrather Port Properties, Ltd. came on board, in the spring of 1983, the Howard Hughes' aircraft, Spruce Goose was purchased and housed in a gigantic geodesic dome astern of the *Queen Mary*. Though this venture cost 22 million dollars, the *Queen Mary*'s ledger showed a profit for the first time in 13 years. This success continued throughout the following years until the Walt Disney Company bought Wrather Corporation for $152,000,000 in March of 1988. Initially, Disney had intentions of developing a 'Disney Sea Park' as an appendage of the Anaheim based amusement park but the *Queen Mary* is a fantastic reality and Disney specialises in realistic fantasias. A rash of news releases echoed a statement that the Disney Corporation had lost 23 million dollars in maintenance and repair. In fact, most of this figure represented expenditures on promotionals and entertainment, not costs incurred by the ship. On September 30,1992, the Port of Long Beach resumed operation of the *Queen Mary* while

Left: *In Sir Winston's Restaurant.*

Disney retreated to its kingdom where all the boats and ships run on tracks.

Contributing to the growing despair was the sale of the Spruce Goose to Evergreen International Aviation Inc. in McMinnville, Oregon. This transaction was finalised almost before the public was made aware and rumours about the *Queen Mary* leaving Long Beach ran rife. Newspapers sensationalised Disney's withdrawal as a surrender, posing the threat, if the Disney Company can't make it work, who can? By the end of 1992, the ship and all associated attractions closed to the public.

After 15 years, the City of Long Beach once again accepted responsibility as owner of the *Queen Mary*. Mr. Joseph F. Prevratil, Chief Executive Office of RMS Foundation, Inc., signed a five year lease as new operator of the property one month after the ship was formally passed into the possession of the city. His organisation, RMS Foundation, Inc., is not to be confused with the preservationist membership of The *Queen Mary* Foundation discussed elsewhere in this book.

On board the *Queen Mary* at the time of this writing, some areas remain little changed from their appearance in 1936 while other portions have undergone entire transformations. The Sports Deck no longer boasts a squash racquet court but a radio room display and an amateur studio for local broadcasts. The electrician's cabins situated above the Verandah Grill have been converted to a Cordon Bleu class restaurant, Sir Winston's. On the Sun Deck, major alterations have taken place. All the cabin-class berths forward of the second expansion joint have been replaced by a vast display area focusing on the ship's role as the Gray Ghost. Just aft of the museum was the Sun Deck Bakery which has recently changed to 'The Boar's Head', a Deli and Bakery. The various accommodations aft are executive offices and the Verandah Grill is a fast food restaurant.

The Promenade Deck has just enough 'patina' to designate it as an antique yet none of the magic has faded. The teak decking and ruboleum at the main entrance have developed a slight hollow from the constant traffic. Twilight brings out the nostalgia in the Mary, most evident in the golden flood of light that welcomes guests into the Promenade Shopping Center at the top of the main staircase. Forward is the popular Observation Lounge. The narrow walkway that once skirted its exterior has been incorporated into the lounge and the colour scheme has been changed from brick red to pale turquoise. Moving along aft in sequence, on the port side, the music studio is currently a tobacco shop, the library is now a showcase for fine crystal and the corner tobacconist is a heraldry store. During the conversion, the funnel hatches were decked over from C-Deck up to the Sports Deck. What used to be the Austin Reed

RMS Mauretania at Rosyth, 4 July 1935.

Shop on the Promenade Deck is now a dress and accessory boutique owned by Mrs. Mary Martin who grew up in Clydebank and remembers watching the progress of job #534! What was the No. 1 funnel hatch is an Art Studio. On the starboard side where the children's playroom was located is a gourmet candy vendor. The drawing room is, appropriately, an art studio and the book store sells camera supplies and postcards.

Just behind the grand staircase where the second funnel hatch was located is the Scottish Heritage merchant. This was formerly the assembly area for guided tours. The writing alcoves bordering this section have been enclosed and serve as additional concessions. Magnificent as in the *Queen Mary*'s sailing days, the cabin-class Main Lounge continues to enchant with Egyptian urn lamps of golden quartzite, frosted light fixtures, peach-tinted mirrors and Maurice Lambert's modeled, gilt unicorns gracing an impressive mural above the simulated fireplace.

The Long and Starboard Galleries have made several transitions, some during the *Queen Mary*'s career at sea. The Long Gallery, famous for the serene paintings, 'Sussex Landscape' and 'Evening on the Avon' became the Amidship's Bar and when the Mary was prepared for her debut in Long Beach, it was selected for the site of a Bank of America. Today, it occupies an area broken into three separate spaces, a T-shirt shop, board room for meetings and hallway into the Chelsea, a buffet style restaurant where the Ballroom used to be. The stretch of Promenade Deck on the starboard side extending from just aft of the main entrance and staircase to a point approximately even with the center of the forward engine hatch, has provided ample room for a duet of restaurants. In the 1970's these were named Lord Nelson's and Lady Hamilton's. The Promenade Cafe, an excellent sandwich and salad restaurant, and the Chelsea have been established in their place. The remainder of the Promenade Deck back to frame 70 has been divided into the 'Victoria Room' and 'King's View Room'; plush banquet or seminar facilities. The Starboard Gallery later was transformed into a cinema and since has been absorbed by the expansion of the Promenade Cafe's kitchen.

The Smoking Room for cabin-class passengers has been preserved and is especially

The beautiful Cabin Class Swimming Pool.

effective for the richly carved panels by James Woodford, sculptured ceiling and lit soffits accentuated by strips of gold hammered-glass above. The Tourist Smoking Room, featuring the beloved painting of the old *Mauritania* on her way to the breaker's yard, became a steak restaurant in the 70's called 'The King's Tavern' and is now The Royal Wedding Chapel.

The Main Deck has been spared from arbitrary changes with the exception of the tourist cocktail bar, known affectionately as 'The Mermaid Bar' and the neighbouring library and writing room. This has been partitioned and is used for storage. The third-class Garden Lounge and appealing Tourist Lounge remain encouragingly intact. On A-Deck, the third-class Smoking Room has been converted into the 'Bow Exhibit' which depicts examples of cabins for each class of passenger. The Tourist Lounge aft serves as a health club for hotel guests and is called 'The Capstan Club'. The old infectious wards under the fantail on B-Deck function as storage space as do the former mail sorting rooms and crew quarters at the extreme bow.

The culmination of architectural design and artistic mastery is celebrated in the sweeping expanses of the ship's Grand Salon on C-Deck. This entire room seems to proclaim the joy of creation and is the site for gala Sunday brunches which offer a variety and quality of cuisine without rival.

The Tourist Dining Room is the employee's cafeteria and nicknamed the "Pig'n'Whistle" after the crew's old bar aft near storage and baggage. The ship's galleys, though modernised, are primarily contained in their original place on C-Deck. The steward's cabins on C and D-Decks are offices and lecture hall for training employees. Forward, in the third-class entrance and dining area, is storage for catering. It is unfortunate that it has not enjoyed the same careful preservation as the third class lounge and cinema one deck above, still brilliant in figured cherry wood and Honduras mahogany.

Ethereal and somewhat mysterious, the cabin-class swimming pool still shimmers, reflecting light from the mother-of-pearl iridescence of its vaulted ceiling. The arches and columns are tiled with champagne-coloured faience and accented with turquoise. The balcony and art-deco sconce lamps impart a theatrical elegance to this hauntingly majestic room.

D-Deck is perhaps the most inherently interesting of decks because of the intricate network of tourist and third-class cabins, crew's quarters, machinery spaces and offices. Most of the original bulkheads have been removed to provide extra footage for the engineering staff's storage, office and repair shop. E-Deck contains only vestiges of its intended uses. Mazes of ladders, fan rooms, uptake and ventilator trunks, auxiliary switchboard cubicles and oil-filling stations mingle with third-class cabins, now distinguishable only by ruboleum companionways running between non-existent bulkheads. Numerous crew areas throughout the vessel are used to store furniture declared surplus.

Between the forward engine room and after turbo-generator room, is a tri-level exhibit hall and convention center that was the Jacques Cousteau Living Sea Museum.

In the 1980's, a maritime museum was composed on D and E-Decks in the vicinity of the after engine room display. Recently included to augment the self-guided engine room tour, is a spectacular film presentation of *The Queen Mary Story*.

At the level of the tanktops in the empty boiler rooms, a perspective of unparalleled drama can be experienced. At one time these caverns were filled with watertube boilers, six in each of four main boiler rooms, and the heaters, strainers and pumps associated with preparing and delivering the fuel and water. The sides of the fuel, overflow and settling tanks are scarred from acetylene torches and streaked with bunker-C fuel residue. Catwalks dangle like steel spiderwebs several decks overhead. Farther forward, in the lonely depths of cargo hold #2, which may be exactly as it had been in 1936, a succession of ascending decks and pillars appear like a rood tower for a steel cathedral. Even the lighting emanating from a vacated upper level gives the impression of a clerestory.

38 feet below the waterline in the dimly illuminated recesses of the world's greatest ship, is an eloquent testimony of the Queen's struggle for survival. Like the mute and solemn form of a church ruined in war, the *Queen Mary*'s boiler rooms are a temple to all dearly bought victories.

Whether viewing the ship from a distance or exploring the innermost secrets, she is the last word in strength and beauty. Like an antebellum mansion, her imposing presence inspires sentiment and reverence for a former time over which she reigned supreme.

Chapter 7

The Queen Mary Foundation
by Diane Rush

The initial motivation to organise a committee to protect the ship was a powerful article appearing in the 1989 volume 13 edition of the Titanic Commutator, the quarterly publication of the Titanic Historic Society. Written by U.S. Marine, D.John Clarkson and entitled, "Inevitable Ship, Inevitable End", the report presented a chronology of the *Queen Mary*'s career as a liner and detailed cases of vandalism and neglect by her management. Reinforced by graphic photographs taken throughout the ship, the list included claims that original furniture and other artefacts were amassed in jumbled heaps on lower decks, uncatalogued and unprotected, and, on the upper decks, lifeboats, decks, and handrails were in a state of deterioration. Tanktops held stagnant water; condensation from air-conditioning units, and it was speculated that the cathodic protection of the ship's outer hull went unregulated. D. John Clarkson concluded his argument by comparing the fate of the *Queen Mary* to that of the *Great Eastern;* the reigning monarch of the seas living out her last days as a carnival ship. Within a few months of this study's publication, the *Queen Mary* Foundation's first board of directors were installed and 150 members on the roster, some from as far away as Australia or South Africa.

Conceived on the premise that the *Queen Mary* requires an advocacy not bound by commercial contract or political loyalties but governed by principles insuring the vessel's preservation and restoration for her own intrinsic worth, the Foundation applied for its articles of incorporation. D.J. Clarkson,

the founder, became the organisation's first president, delivering addresses on the ship's behalf at fundraisers and conventions.

In 1990, The *Queen Mary* Foundation was officially registered as a 501-C-3, the designation given to a non-profit entity. The inaugural edition of the organisation's newsletter, *The Guardian,* was distributed in the spring of 1991 which contained articles and correspondence by Captain John Treasure Jones and C.W.R. Winter. With endorsements such as these, we were off to a good start.

In subsequent newsletters, The *Queen Mary* Foundation had much to denounce regarding the lack of forethought executed in the operation of the ship by the Walt Disney Company. 'French Line' red was selected to repaint the vessel's funnels, much to the consternation of maritime buffs who felt insulted that the *Queen Mary* was forced to don the color of Cunard's major competitor. Nothing, however, so incensed the members of our foundation as the removal of after docking machinery on the ship's fantail in 1991. The steering gear skylight, warping winch, capstans, capstan controllers, bollards, fairleads, mushroom vents and a pair of ladders were stripped from the deck, altering the ship's profile. This action was especially wasteful because it was to make room for the installation of an outdoor swimming pool which was later discovered not to be feasible. All of the portside Promenade Deck windows were replaced by permanent plexiglass, and, once again, it was recognised after the fact to be in error. During summer months this area needs ventilation. Had the management consulted with their historian, they would have learned the original windows were fitted with frames that allowed raising and lowering. In the Main Lounge one of the quartzite urns has lost a small section of its rim. Instead of having a new piece fashioned, a beige plastic rectangle backed with newsprint to "give it texture" is utilised. Mahogany headboards in the staterooms have been upholstered with turquoise snakeskin naugahyde, fastened by 1/2" staples.

On March 6, 1992, the Port and City of Long Beach received notice that the lease of the *Queen Mary* and surrounding properties was to be discontinued by the Disney Company. Disney agreed to manage the ship until September 30,1992, at which time the Port would assume all responsibilities until another operator with a viable proposal was selected. All hotel and banquet facilities ceased at the end of September however, the *Queen Mary* tours resumed until the last day of 1992.

"A Queen in Peril" was the headline banner across the front of *The Guardian* issued in the Spring of 1992, scarcely a year after

the foundation had drafted its bylaws. This study authored by D.J. Clarkson, *"In Order to Scrap a Legend"*, was in response to the Port of Long Beach offering to sell their city's icon. Clarkson analysed the prospect of the *Queen Mary* being sold for scrap based on statistics obtained from the Steamship and Railway Heritage Trust of Seattle, Washington. According to his findings, the *Queen Mary* had a 10 million dollar scrap value but it would cost at least 46 million to remove the asbestos, assure her seaworthiness with structural reinforcements and to tow her to the breaker.

Just as in 1967 when Cunard was considering bids for the two Queens, the Port of Long Beach reviewed the same number of prospective buyers, 18 in all. This seems a modest response until you realise that each offer had to be backed by 100,000 dollars just to have their proposal considered! By mid-September of 1992, the choice had been narrowed to 6 contenders. Two bidders were from Japanese firms, one from Hong Kong, another from Southampton and a fifth from Joseph F. Prevratil who had previous experience with the ship under the management of

One small section of the 810,730 troops she carried in WWII (David F. Hutchings).

the Wrather Port Properties. A sixth offer, never identified by the press but was widely believed to have been a proposal to scrap the vessel or otherwise destroy her, was also evaluated. The media had a ready source of sensational and controversial news about the *Queen Mary* and may have inadvertently assisted her preservation through their agitating declarations. One Long Beach paper issued on September 20, 1992, ran an article with the heading, *"Queen: Once-glamorous luxury liner has become royal pain for Long Beach"*. While some residents may have accepted such statements passively, the majority of the citizens were outraged. The Harbor Commission had established a reputation advocating the sale of the ship to foreign interests and it was speculated that the Port of Long Beach was determined to expand the freighter terminal to encompass Pier J where the *Queen Mary* is berthed.

The *Queen Mary* Foundation was primed for the first campaign to save the ship. All during the summer of 1992, the *Queen Mary*'s advocates attended Harbor Commission meetings and assemblies of the Long Beach City Council. When issues involving the fate of the *Queen Mary* were on the agenda, we packed the chambers and kept vigils, frequently around the clock. We developed a sophisticated network to transmit information to our supporters and knew when and where to concentrate our strength to effect political decisions and seek representation in media coverage. The Port Building and City Council were flooded with letters and petitions from those wishing to keep the *Queen Mary* in Long Beach. The efforts of The *Queen Mary* Foundation were greatly augmented by veterans, employees of the ship, business owners and other individuals willing to demonstrate their commitment. When the media attended those critical assemblies, our speeches were televised and quoted by the press. People from the east coast of the United States and from across the Atlantic registered their convictions before Harbor Commission and City Council. Some of us never missed a rally, media event, Port or Council meeting. We were resolved to do what was necessary to persuade the city administra-

L.B. council OKs lease of Queen Mary

By Sharon Hormell
Staff writer

It's been a roller coaster ride for the Queen Mary/A6

LONG BEACH — Discounting the city auditor's warning that the deal was underfinanced, the City Council unanimously voted Tuesday to lease the Queen Mary to a nonprofit group headed by Joseph Prevratil.

Prevratil, who once ran the ship when it was leased by the Wrather Corp., said he would sign the lease this week and would open the ship tours and a couple of restaurants next week.

The City Council vote triggered a triumphant celebration by more than 100 former Queen Mary workers attending the meeting.

"Joe! Joe! Joe!" they chanted in the crowded council chamber. They clapped, whistled and shouted, and scores of people waved signs (on which his name was misspelled) that said: "We support Joe Previtril."

After the meeting, Rosendo Caldera, a banquet waiter who was laid off in October after 14 years and who nearly lost his property in a foreclosure, rushed to Prevratil and shook his hand.

"Let's go clean now," Caldera said. "Whenever they are ready, I will volunteer to clean the place so we can get to work fast."

Prevratil said, "It's the employees and people who are associated with the Queen Mary who have kept the faith throughout this long vigil, and I am very appreciative of that."

Prevratil's financial backer, FHP Inc. founder and chairman Dr. Robert Gumbiner, said he will give $2 million to the nonprofit RMS Foundation Inc., which will run the ship.

The council agreed to waive a requirement that the foundation also post a $3 million loan guarantee within 30 days as the original lease proposal required.

Instead, Gumbiner agreed to help raise that amount or more

PLEASE SEE QUEEN/A6

Enter Joe Prevratil.

tors that we all needed the *Queen Mary*. One individual flew to California from New Jersey for the express purpose of speaking out to save the *Queen Mary*, and one vacationing couple on their honeymoon forfeited an entire day to speak for three minutes on why it was crucial to preserve the beloved landmark.

The fervour reached a crescendo during the 28th and 29th of September during which time the City of Long Beach would vote to either reclaim the ship from the Port authorities or allow the Harbor Commission to retain its jurisdiction. In a 48 hour continuous debate, a band of loyal proponents stayed in the Port Building and then pursued the contest at the City Council chamber the next day. Some of us did not eat or sleep for this period of time for the privilege of speaking a precious 6 minutes. On the night of September 29, 1992, the City Council of Long Beach resolved the debate in a 7 - 2 vote to keep the *Queen Mary* and to assume ownership for the first time in 14 years. Long Beach reclaimed their 534! Amid the shouts and tears of joy we decided to celebrate this victory at the *Queen Mary*, in her beautiful Observation Lounge Bar.

The battle was not over, as circumstances soon made evident. Only 3 days after a resounding victory, the tables appeared to be turned again. A marine surveying firm, Rados Corporation, had released a report that the *Queen Mary*'s shaft tunnels were severely oxidised and the interior plates and rivets in the prop bossings were in an advanced state of deterioration, allowing seepage of sea water. It was asserted that the gland packings also were not water tight and presented a threat of progressive leaking. Removal of bulkheads between boiler room 1 and 2 and between 3 and 4 as well as other structural modifications rendered some areas vulnerable to undue stresses, according to Rados. Improperly maintained decks allowed moisture to accumulate between the steel and teakwood planks, further endangering the ship, Rados diagnosed. Port officials said they could not, in good conscience, allow a vessel in this condition to pass from their immediate control. This delayed further decisions and cast uncertainty on the prospect of Long Beach signing the agreement with the Port.

Time seemed to be running out. The Disney employees, cut down to a minimum operating staff of 400, faced unemployment by the end of December and over 1,000 of their compatriots had already experienced this fate. To add to the confusion, the Port decreed that Long Beach had until October 26 to take possession of the ship or else all bids would be thrown out and the process of request proposals would begin anew.

Gambling in Long Beach to create another source of revenue was an issue to appear on the November ballot and some suggested turning part of the *Queen Mary*'s exhibit hall

into a casino. The Port may have viewed this as a viable solution for they consented to postpone the transferral of the vessel until this measure was voted on. Proposition J, the initiative for gambling on the *Queen Mary* premises, was voted down.

Another turning point in the political maze occurred on October 20, during a session at the City Council meeting. Earlier that day, a report by the U.S. Navy contradicting the Rados findings, was printed in the Long Beach papers. The *Queen Mary* issue on the agenda was shuffled back until after dinner, a circumstance we had become resigned to. When it came time for the public addresses, Hal Johnson, former diver for the City of Long Beach and technician for the cathodic protection system of the *Queen Mary* gave his report and video presentation which substantiated the U.S. Navy data and repudiated the more negative assertions made by Rados. However, it must be noted that the questions put to the Rados surveying company involved speculations on worst case scenarios for the purpose of insurance and safety regulations. The Rados reports did not imply what was probable but what was possible given certain conditions. This is where the misleading statements were derived insinuating the vessel was in danger of sinking. Hal Johnson's video was a tour of the shaft tunnels showing that the areas in doubt were dry and intact although showing superficial oxidation.

A former executive of the Wrather Corporation, Richard Kierstein, gave a financial report detailing the liner's impressive profit history. His thorough analysis of the Disney Corporation's expenditures and return on investment showed a huge profit margin. Kierstein's scrutiny of a plan by Long Beach to invest 95 million dollars in the expansion of the convention center projected that, without the *Queen Mary* in the harbor, promoters and contractors would take their business elsewhere causing the convention complex and hotels of Long Beach to suffer a dramatic loss of patronage. This assertion was based on actual cases where conventions were cancelled and bids withdrawn by those contractors who believed the *Queen Mary* would be leaving Long Beach.

Not only marine surveyors and financial analysts concurred with the Foundation's position but maritime associations such as

FULL STEAM AHEAD

Board the Queen Mary – *FREE!*
Reopening Friday, February 26

Make History! The Queen Mary is back! Now you and your family can come aboard the Long Beach landmark liner **FREE OF CHARGE!**

Historic Tours. Pick up a free map, and tour the ship on your own, or sign up at Passenger Information on Promenade Deck for guided tours departing daily from 10 a.m. until 4 p.m. The guided tour is only $5.00 for adults and $3.00 for children 2-11.

On Board Dining. Enjoy lunch or dinner served daily at the elegant Sir Winston's or the more casual Promenade Cafe. The Observation Bar, with its panoramic views of the Long Beach skyline, is the place for friends to gather Fridays and Saturdays from 4:30 p.m. Beginning Saturday, your choice for a quick bite to eat might be The Verandah Grill, the Sundeck Bakery or a number of other convenient locations.

Sunday Brunch. The spectacular Queen Mary Sunday Brunch resumes February 28 with seatings from 10 a.m. to 2 p.m. Make reservations now at special introductory prices of $19.93 for adults and $9.93 for children 2-11.

Hotel Staterooms Only $49.00. To celebrate the reopening of the Hotel Queen Mary on March 5, and continuing through Labor Day, a limited number of staterooms are being offered daily starting as low as $49.00 per night, plus tax, based on availability.

Banquets, Weddings, Receptions & Conferences. The Queen Mary is now accepting reservations for ceremonies in the Royal Wedding Chapel, banquets and receptions, business conferences, whatever your special event might be. Call Monday through Friday, 8:30 a.m. to 5:00 p.m.

THE QUEEN MARY.
(310) 435-3511

Boarding hours February 26 through March 4 from 10 a.m. daily. Tour hours from 10 a.m. to 6 p.m. daily. Restaurant hours vary. Hotel begins partial operation March 5 and resumes full operation April 5. Parking, $3.00 per vehicle, $5.00 overside. Children must be accompanied by an adult. Located at the South end of the Long Beach (710) Freeway in the Port of Long Beach.

the U.S. Merchant Marine Veterans of World War II. This organisation has served as mentor to The _Queen Mary_ Foundation, proving repeatedly that miracles can be achieved through expert volunteer services. The Vice President, John O. Smith, was also the Chief Operations Engineer on the _Queen Mary_ during her final voyage. Through the dedication of the members of the U.S. Merchant Marine Veterans of World War II, the maritime community of Long Beach has been tremendously enriched. The primary contribution was the total restoration of the Lane Victory, a merchant cargo ship built in 1945. This vessel arrived in San Pedro, a derelict hulk, in 1989 and today is designated a National Historic Landmark and provides regular cruises to Catalina, off the South California Coast.

For months The _Queen Mary_ Foundation had been urging members and interested parties to write to the California State Office of Historic Preservation to nominate the _Queen Mary_ as a candidate for the National Register of Historic Places. The advantages conferred by this status include tax reduction, governmental funding for certain types of restoration projects and a measure of protection from significant alterations in addition to the recognition and honor bestowed by this title. The President and Treasurer of The _Queen Mary_ Foundation, David Rubin and Cherry Cook, went to Sacramento to speak before the State Historic Resources Commission on November 6, 1992. Some of the _Queen Mary_'s many qualifications are:

1. The _Queen Mary_'s role as a transport carrier in World War II. She could carry an entire military division and transported a total of 800,000 troops during the war. On a crossing in 1943 she carried the largest number of people ever recorded on a vessel, 16,683!
2. The _Queen Mary_ is the only ship of her design and the last of her genre of transatlantic luxury liners. Her heritage includes the combined glory of the two most famous shipping lines in history, the Cunard and White Star Lines.
3. The ship is acclaimed as being the finest example of Art-Deco nautical architecture and interior design.
4. The _Queen Mary_ represents a cultural and diplomatic bridge between America and Great Britain.
5. This picturesque vessel is an established landmark of the City of Long Beach which symbolises a history of shipbuilding, industry and commerce.

These are just a few of the reasons the Cunarder merits National Register status. The _Queen Mary_ Foundation will be engaged in a continual effort to raise the standards of protection afforded to the liner and pursue the goal of having her declared a National Historic Landmark and eventually, an International Monument.

The supreme moment of triumph for our organisation came on April 15, 1993 when the _Queen Mary_ was officially admitted to the National Register of Historic Places. The bronze plaque awarded by the Foundation is inscribed "R.M.S. _Queen Mary_ has been placed on the National Register of Historic Places by the United States Department of the Interior".

While members of The _Queen Mary_ Foundation were being notified of this accomplishment, I was on the second of two trips to Great Britain to rally support and explore possibilities for having former _Queen Mary_ engineers, shipwrights and crew members visit their ship in Southern California. The sentimental climate was favourable; the next stage was to cultivate enthusiasm on my own side of the Atlantic.

It was also my intention to inspire an interest in the development of a consociation between Clydebank, Scotland and Long Beach, Californa, with the option of establishing Sister Cityhood between the two communities. The basis for this cultural bond includes the following:

1. Both cities were established by the shipbuilding industry. The Clyde produced some 36,000 vessels which averages a ship a day for 100 years.
2. During the Second World War, Clydebank and Long Beach produced significant percentages of the naval vessels and armaments for their respective nations.

United States Department of the Interior

NATIONAL PARK SERVICE
P.O. Box 37127
Washington, D.C. 20013-7127

IN REPLY REFER TO:
(413)

MAY 10 1993

David R. Rubin
Chairman
Queen Mary Foundation
7 Verdugo Boulevard
Canada, CA 91011

Dear Mr. Rubin:

We received your letter of April 8, 1993, regarding the
nomination of the R.M.S. Queen Mary to the National Register of
Historic Places. We are pleased to tell you that the property
was listed in the National Register on April 15, 1993.

We appreciate your interest in the National Register program.
Should you have any questions about this, please contact Toni Lee
of the National Register staff at (202) 343-9520.

Sincerely,

Carol D. Shull

Carol D. Shull
Chief of Registration
National Register of Historic Places
Interagency Resources Division

Another historic milestone in her life.

3. Tourist trade is on the increase, offering an alternative source of revenue to the traditionally industrial cities. Both Clydebank and Long Beach represent a blend of history, art and industry.
4. The *Queen Mary* symbolises a shared heritage and could provide a dramatic publicity site for annual celebrations.

It wasn't until December 22, 1992, after weeks of vacillation by the Harbor Commission and sensational press coverage that the City of Long Beach was finally named owner of the *Queen Mary* and associated property. Joseph F. Prevratil's financial plan was accepted and on January 27, 1993, the lease was signed and the new operator took over management.

Still, the ship remained closed to the public until February 26, 1993. On that morning, at dawn, a crowd gathered beside the ship in eager anticipation, reminiscent of an April day in Clydebank back in 1934. It may seem an exaggeration to state that many locals were melancholy about the two month closure of the *Queen Mary*. In a culture of high tension and impermanence, the ship has become an institution combining the otherwise absent functions of church, pub, ancestral estate and castle ruin. Several times I visited the ship during this period, often in driving rain. On each occasion, I met others who came for similar reasons. One day in particular was memorable for the stormy weather and number of people who turned out. Most of us had umbrellas, although the shelter they afford on such days is negligible. We each found our own vantage point in the parking lot beside the towering vessel and gazed upon her form in silence. The poetic urge flourishes under these conditions and it was only when the paper I began writing verses on had become papier maché that I finally decided to turn back for home.

During the summer of 1993, The *Queen Mary* Foundation had concerns about the proposal to implement a shoreline development project called the Queensway Bay Plan. One version of the plan called for using Pier J as a cruise terminal and transforming the opposite shoreline to an aquatic theme park. It was suggested that the *Queen Mary* would have to be moved to the base of Pine Avenue. The hazards and expenses would have ruled out that option in the first stages of a feasibility study. Parts of the harbor would have to be dredged, the rock berm enclosing the ship which cost over 1 million to install would have to be removed, the ship's orientation would be reversed, necessitating the penetration of the starboard hull for entry ways and utility connections. Furthermore, funnels and other rigid structural alterations would make the move difficult, not to mention the drag which would result from the propeller viewing box encasing her port outboard prop. These and other considerations would expose the ship to dangers that outweigh any advantages to be gained by the move. Fortunately, after hearing objections from our Foundation, ship's employees and various individuals, the City

Council voted the issue down.

The *Queen Mary* Foundation has its own office on board the ship and has future plans of working with the exhibits department in establishing a reference library for visitors to the *Queen Mary*. The archives collected by our Foundation and items already donated by our members will be among the available material for research and photocopying.

Various departments of administration on the *Queen Mary* have co-operated with The *Queen Mary* Foundation, accepting several of our proposals, which, in turn, increase revenue for the ship. The 59th Anniversary Celebration of the *Queen Mary*'s Launch, reprinting of "Queen Mary: Her Early Years Recalled" and Sister City project were efforts pioneered by our organisation. Plans are on the drawing board for the 60th Anniversary Celebration which show great promise and have already generated much enthusiasm. Maintaining overseas contacts with Britons affiliated with the *Queen Mary* and other historic vessels has provided an endless wealth of information, assistance and encouragement.

Our volunteer hours have also contributed to the organising of plan rooms which contain engineer's blueprints on board the *Queen Mary*. On display in the maritime museum on D-Deck is the original cabin class purser's safe on loan from The *Queen Mary* Foundation. Short range goals include restoration of the cabin class swimming pool and Long Gallery for hotel guests' use.

Currently, The *Queen Mary* Foundation is working with the exhibits co-ordinator to

Mary Magnificent

For thirty-one years you have sailed the Atlantic,
A magic blue circle your pasture,
In fair weather, foul weather, wind blowing frantic,
Surviving a war of disaster.

Age has not scarred you or sullied your beauty,
Your stamina knows no decay,
And your thirty-knot speed is as much as you need
To compete with the best of today.

You've carried the famous, the infamous too,
And those unattuned to the sea,
And hordes of just everyday, commonplace folk,
Nonentity people like me.

But you'll soon be retired as no longer required,
For you're uneconomic they say,
Your friends are all horrified, Mary old girl,
But sentiment won't pay your way.

So you and Q.E. must abandon the sea,
But passengers now in their teens,
As time passes by will recount with a sigh,
The legend of Cunard's two Queens.

Mrs. C. G

'Mary Magnificent'.

design a display to honour the shipbuilders of John Brown's shipyard which will feature a three-dimensional model of the shipyard with buildings, cranes, fitting-out basin and launching ways. Photographs, artefacts and a 20 minute audio track will accompany this exciting project.

Several long range goals are in consideration such as the recreation of boiler room #3. The Foundation promotes any idea that fosters interaction and discovery while on board or restores authenticity to the ship.

Chapter 8

The Glorious 59th Anniversary

This is a personal account of what was a truly glorious happening, the celebration aboard the *Queen Mary* of the 59th anniversary of her launching and christening on 26th September 1934 by Queen Mary herself. It was a happening that I was privileged to be a part of, to join in with, and in a very small way to contribute to. For my wife and I the festivities lasted a full week of our visit, every waking moment of which was crammed with interest. It was, in the words of Lady Bracknell, a life crowded with incident, and our feet barely seemed to touch the deck.

For us the celebrations all began at Gatwick Airport in London where we were met by Lisa Lynn Backus who had flown to Europe expressly to collect and shepherd the *Queen Mary*'s guests on this occasion. Lisa, an intrepid traveller if ever there was one, had already been to Scotland to collect John Brown, the designer, and his niece Christine Schmitt Mackinnon, George Kean, the shipwright, and his wife Betty, and Provost Alastair MacDonald of Clydebank. At Gatwick she added to the party my wife Patricia and myself, my son Anthony and his wife Daphne, to complete the group, most of whom were visiting Long Beach for the first time.

The first leg of our flight, to Dallas in Texas, was in an American Airlines Boeing 767, a very comfortable aircraft. The Cabin Staff were attentive, the food good and the service excellent, but the flight itself was long and tiring. We were late in take-off, and as there were strong westerly winds blowing over the North Atlantic we flew north instead of west. Indeed, we heard several days later that the *Q.E.2* had run into a severe gale in crossing the Atlantic, which was an apposite reminder of the difference between sea and air travel, for while she had been tossing about down below we had been sitting in the calm comfort of our huge air liner.

Firstly we flew over Glasgow, which must have been a little irritating to our five Glaswegians who had just come from there, then over Iceland, then Greenland, and then down over Canada. For the first part of this leg, flying at 35,000 feet, we saw nothing of the earth for we were high above a thick layer of cloud, but over Canada there were gaps in the cloud cover and we caught some fascinating glimpses of the countryside, including the Great Lakes.

RON AND HIS FAMILY ARE COMIN' TAE SEE ME!

Diane Rush

Left: *Arrival at Long Beach Airport from Britain.*
L-R: *Provost Alastair Macdonald of Clydebank, John Brown, Designer, George Kean, Shipwright, Ron Winter, Author, Alan Lowenthal, City Councilman.*
Middle Left: *Our destination*
Bottom Left: *The sweep of the bridge.*
Right: *Some of her ten million rivets.*

At Dallas Airport we were met by an official of American Airlines complete with an electric buggy, and he transported us to the main airline building for our next flight to Long Beach. Actually we had quite a long wait for we were late in arriving and had missed our connection. He escorted us to a passenger lounge where we were able to relax, and I personally had the pleasure of meeting an old friend, Bob Lenzer, who lives in Texas and had taken the trouble to come in and meet us.

Bob Lenzer is one of a number of young Americans who can only be described as *Queen Mary* fanatics. It has always been a source of great amazement to me, and a matter for considerable gratitude, that so many young people in America who were not even born when the *Queen Mary* was in her heyday, should be so passionately devoted to the ship and her welfare. Bob is one of these, one of several who have spent not only their spare time but their hard earned cash in visiting Britain to see exactly where she was built, where she operated from, and to meet some of the people who had been involved with her in her early days. On these 'pilgrimages' many of them have found their way to the Isle of Wight, and it has been my great pleasure and privilege to meet with them there.

As you will have read in a previous chapter the *Queen Mary* Foundation was set up by a number of these devotees, and with so much dedication and determination around it is difficult to see how the ship can fail to be a success. These qualities of single mindedness and sheer devotion to the *Queen Mary*'s welfare are striking in the extreme, but have not always been appreciated by the ship's owners and operators. But this fund of enthusiasm must surely constitute a powerful source of energy that could and should, be put to good use. Maybe on occasion the Foundation's eagerness to help has overstepped itself, and has been regarded by the

ship's management as an irritant, but with tolerance and understanding it can be channelled and usefully employed. And there is an old saying that one volunteer is worth two pressed men.

Our little party was met at Long Beach Airport at 9 p.m. by an impressive reception committee, consisting of City Councilman Alan Lowenthal, Diane Rush, President of the *Queen Mary* Foundation, Maria DuBry and Jessica Linde, Assistants to Lisa Lynn Backus, and Lisa's husband Dick who is the City's Traffic Manager. They whisked us off to the ship in a private coach, the chatter of conversation and laughter filling the night air. As the *Queen Mary* first came into view across the harbour, floodlit and serene, silence descended on us all and a tape of Roger Whittaker singing 'The Last Farewell', one of George Kean's favourite songs, was played. This was a very kind thought and it certainly was an emotional moment, for those of us who knew her had not seen her for over 50 years, and several members of our party had never before seen her at all.

Once we were aboard the ship the excitement can be imagined. We were conducted to our cabins on Main Deck, tiredness temporarily disappeared, and we all met a few minutes later in the Promenade Cafe for a final drink before retiring. Alas, for some of us sleep was out of the question, and for me personally the feelings that welled up were quite overwhelming. This ship had at one time not only been my workplace but my home, and indeed my whole life, and to return to her after all these years was an incredible experience. I did not know whether to laugh or to cry, so in the end with a little of each, I went to bed.

The following morning saw the start of a week in which events came thick and fast, and all were exciting. To my family everything was new, strange, and interesting. To me, the nostalgia of my surroundings coupled with the excitement of the occasion were sufficient to prevent me from sleeping for more than three hours on any night. I presume the deficiency was made up by the adrenaline that was flowing in large quantities.

In the wakeful hours I had plenty of time to think and to realise that there were three people who were particularly to be thanked for our presence here aboard the ship. The whole idea was dreamed up by Diane Rush, and I believe she got a certain satisfaction in seeing her dream come true. Praise is also

Above: *Ron Winter and John Brown on a tour of the ship. On the right Roy Sorge, one of the ship's officers can just be seen.*
Right: *Ernie Kell, Mayor of Long Beach, Joseph F. Prevratil, and Provost Alastair MacDonald.*
Far Right: *Watching the presentations. From L to R: John Brown, George Kean, Betty Kean, Christine McKinnon (John Brown's niece), Ron Winter, Alan Lowenthal.*
Bottom Right: *Centrepiece of the Sunday Champagne Brunch. Magnificent, and worth travelling a long way for!*

due, and must be given, to Lisa Lyn Backus of Pacifica Speciality Tours, who as the *Queen Mary*'s Special Events Organiser, was responsible for all the arrangements throughout the week. Her organisation was superb. Lisa had already been to Europe to collect her guests, and must have been more tired than any of us, but of this she gave no sign. She issued to each one of us a programme of events, and every morning an updated and detailed itinerary for the day. It was all very helpful and efficient. The third person to whom we were indebted is of course Joe Prevratil who made the visit possible.

The programme was intriguing and full of interest, much thought having gone into the task of making our visit both rewarding to us and useful to the ship. John Brown was quite naturally the star of the show. As an important member of the original design team who created the *Queen Mary* he was much in demand, and at 92 his stamina and the way he coped with a very exacting programme

was quite remarkable. George Kean was also very much in the spotlight, and I have already quoted the excellent address he gave on the Sunday morning. My own modest contribution was to talk to some of the Staff on Saturday morning about life aboard the ship in her early days, and to give a slide presentation to the assembled company of visitors immediately preceding the Sunday Brunch. Also of course to supply copies of my book "Queen Mary: Her Early Years Recalled" which had been reprinted especially to mark the occasion.

On Sunday 26th September, the actual 59th anniversary of the launch, the programme was as follows -

10 a.m. Panel Discussions:
"Mosaic of Memories: from Design and Launch to the First and Last Voyages." (Held in the Queens Salon - the original First Class Lounge)

> Moderator:
> Dr. Alan Lowenthal: Long Beach City Councilman
> Panellists:
> John Brown: Naval Architect and *Queen Mary* Designer.

George Kean: *Queen Mary*
Shipwright.
Ron Winter: Author and ex-*Queen Mary* Electrical Officer
Jack Webster: Editor, Glasgow Herald.
Dr. Thomas Clark: Long Beach Councilman.

11 a.m. A Procession was formed, and led by Bagpipers, proceeded to the ship's bow. The Ceremony on the Foredeck consisted of -

Speeches by: Joseph F. Prevratil: President and C.E.O. R.M.S Foundation Inc.
Diane Rush: President *Queen Mary* Foundation, who presented a commemorative plaque to Mr. Prevratil.
Ernie Kell: Mayor of Long Beach, who referred to the Sister City Project and made a presentation to -
Provost Alastair Macdonald: who responded to Mayor Kell and made presentations to him and to Mr. Prevratil.
Mike Murchison, from Supervisor Deane Dana's Office, who also made a presentation.
Mervyn T.Jones: Deputy British Consul General.
John Brown, who presented Mr. Prevratil with the original drafting instruments used in the first designs.
George Kean was then escorted by two Ship's Officers to the Ship's Bell, which he rang 59 times.

12 noon The Ship's Siren was sounded, and an Airship flew overhead. The winner of the fund raising draw was announced and then the Procession was reformed and led by the Bagpipers proceeded to the Windsor Salon.

12.15 p.m. Travis Montgomery, Director of Developments, introduced Ron Winter who gave a slide show about life in the *Queen Mary* in her early days.

Following this last presentation the normal Sunday Champagne Brunch was taken.

The ceremony on the foredeck was conducted in a very friendly atmosphere but also managed to be impressive, and I think we were all - both British and Americans - thrilled with the thought of Long Beach and Clydebank being 'twinned'. Provost Alastair Macdonald and Mayor Ernie Kell impressed everyone with their sincerity and enthusiasm for the project, and there is no doubt that this contributed greatly to the happiness of the occasion. For my part, perhaps the most satisfying feature of the day was the public evidence of the friendly co-operation between the ship's operators, R.M.S. Foundation Inc, and the amateur organisation The *Queen Mary* Foundation. This is a 'Pro-Am' collaboration that can only benefit the ship, for both the professionals who depend on her for their livelihood, and the amateurs who have dedicated themselves to her preservation, have exactly the self-same goal.

Together they represent a powerful and irresistible force.

In our week's itinerary several excursions had been thoughtfully arranged for us so that we might see something of Long Beach and district other than the *Queen Mary* herself, and there were several periods of free time. Rather ungraciously I begged to be excused from some of these events for there was so much I wanted to see in the ship, and I knew that one week was never going to be long enough. Robin Jacobs and Bill Cwiklow both spent a lot of time showing me round and helping me to remember places that I once knew but which were now completely changed.

One such place was in Sir Winston's Restaurant which occupies a position on top of the Verandah Grill. This had once been Engineers' accommodation, and Diane Rush had some time previously kindly sent me photographs of it. Now it happened that I knew the exact position of my cabin on this deck, for part of the mainmast went up through the back of the wardrobe that stood at the foot of my bunk. And as the mainmast is visible in Sir Winston's I was able to pinpoint the exact spot where I had slept (or not) so many years ago. A silly thing perhaps, but fascinating nevertheless.

Away from the ship three events in my week's visit stand out and will remain in my memory. The first of these was a tour of Long Beach Harbor arranged by Hal Johnson with his friend Van in the latter's fine fishing cruiser 'The Spoiler'. This was fascinating in the extreme and was, I believe,

primarily organised for the benefit of my son Anthony who had been in shipping all his adult life and had for some time been Chief Executive of a Group of Shipping Companies in the U.K. The weather could not have been more perfect, and Travis Montgomery, who knows the Port as well as anybody, gave Tony and I a running commentary on the way.

Later we were given another and equally interesting tour of the Port operation, organised by Lisa Lynn Backus and conducted by Steven Macias, Special Events Manager for the Port of Long Beach. On this occasion we were taken out in a Fire Float and saw at first hand the working of the Fire Department. This was a public relations exercise of the first order.

The third event that I shall long remember

was a visit to a meeting of the City Council by invitation from Mayor Ernie Kell. Here we were graciously received and introduced to the Council, and some very kind remarks were made by the Mayor about the *Queen Mary* and our visit.

Apart from the above there seemed to be an unending list of things I wanted to do and people I wanted to meet, and there were just not enough hours in the day nor days in the week. Several old friends came aboard to see me and it was disappointing not to have more time to catch up on their news. Alas the time passed all too quickly, and before we knew where we were it was Thursday, 30th September and we were due to fly home. We were seen off at Long Beach Airport by several of our new found friends, and in many ways it was a rather sad little party that embarked in an American Airlines Jet for the long flight to England.

The journey home was completed without a hitch, the comfort and attention of the American Airlines Staff was superb, and the food served was of gourmet standard. When we landed at Gatwick Airport in London it was, perhaps inevitably, raining, so that we came down to earth both literally and metaphorically. I think all of us during the next week or so suffered, not only from the problems of jet lag, but also from those of hospitality lag.

Top Left: *Aboard Van's beautiful yacht which took us around the harbour.*

Left, centre: *Steven Macias, Special Events Manager, Port of Long Beach.*

Left: *The final photograph as the British visitors prepared to leave for the Airport. L to R: Tony Winter, Hal Johnson, Betty Kean, Pat Winter, John Brown, Christine McKinnon, Diane Rush, Maria DuBry, Ron Winter, Jessica Linde, Daphne Winter, Lisa Lynne Backus, Dick Backus, George Kean.*

Chapter 9

A Queen at the Crossroads

This chapter should perhaps start with a disclaimer, for in it you may think that I am trying to teach my grandmother how to suck eggs. But this is very far from the metaphorical truth, and it must be stated quite plainly that the opinions about to be expressed are not an attempt to interfere in the management of the ship, nor even to advise anyone in any position of authority on how to do their job. No, my opinions are merely those of an outsider with an abiding love of the *Queen Mary*, but who carries absolutely no responsibility for her economic viability. My background is such that in my early twenties I worked and lived for nearly three years aboard the *Queen Mary*, a sufficient time to give me a lifelong devotion to the ship, a devotion that incidentally I am now more than happy to share with many many younger people.

This affection however does not give me a special insight into the many problems which must be associated with running this mammoth business undertaking, and I have nothing but humble admiration for those who have taken it on. But love is a great motivator, and the urge to form opinions, and to give them expression in print, is irrepressible. Many of the ideas that have been put forward, and will be put forward, and which I find interesting and exciting may, and in all probability will,

be dubbed impractical. But Henry Ford, in one of his books, taught me, a long time ago, not to dwell on all the reasons why it was impossible to do a particular thing, and just to concentrate on how to do it. And to accentuate the positive and eliminate the negative has always seemed to me to be a pretty sound formula for success.

Following my visit to Long Beach in September 1993 I came to a number of conclusions, and would like to share some of these with you. It was bewilderingly apparent that over the years she had been in Long Beach a multitude of alterations had taken place, many of which may have been part of some grand major plan, but which nevertheless now give the appearance of being haphazard and uncoordinated. Twenty six years is of course a long time, and in it managers can come and go. All managers and operators can be expected to have their own pet theories and schemes for making money, and so it is hardly surprising to find considerable changes in the layout of the vessel as this plan and that plan were tried in a desperate attempt to achieve economic success.

Changes such as, for example, the scrapping of the original and unique propulsion machinery. It is difficult now to understand the thinking behind this decision, for surely if a 'Museum of the Sea' is required then the *Queen*

24 March 1936. Stern first she leaves her birthplace. Her first movement as a complete ship ready for the sea.

Mary's propulsion equipment would have made a splendid starting point. It was puzzling over this that forced me to the conclusion that in her early days at Long Beach no one was interested in her as a ship and the symbol of an era that was coming to an end. Her principal asset to her new owners was the world-wide publicity she brought with her, and her interest to an operator was as an unusually shaped building in which he could do his own thing. This is borne out by the fact that she was soon de-registered as a ship and classed as a building. Indeed, I think it is possible to go further than this and say that until the present management took her over no operator has been in the least interested in exploiting her as the last and possibly greatest relic of a bygone form of transport.

In my view this is the only logical explanation for the wholesale changes that were made in her first few Long Beach years, changes that with hindsight we may perhaps be excused now for listing them under the heading of appalling damage. As we look round the ship today and see not only the enormous spaces that once housed the boiler rooms, generating stations, and forward engine room, but also the loss of such first class public rooms as the Long Gallery and the Ballroom, the abandonment of much of the Third Class accommodation, the mutilation of parts of the Promenade Deck, desecration of the Verandah Grill, etc. etc. the initial feeling is one of despair. At first sight much of it would seem to be irreparable, the damage far too great for it to be possible ever to return to her former magnificence.

If anyone should still claim that the changes that were made - at astronomical expense - were justified, let them just take a walk through some of the areas I have listed above, for they will find them empty, devoid of activity, not producing a single cent of the desperately needed revenue that must be generated to make the business successful.

Let them visit, for example, the original Main Tourist Lounge, a large and magnificent room, but empty. Let them look for Bertram Nicholls once famous painting "A Sussex Landscape", a painting that any Art Gallery in the world would be proud to exhibit, for as I have said in a previous chapter, they will find it covered by a large mod-

The Bronze Cowboy. Part of her pre-war finery. (University Archives, University of Liverpool).

Part of a frieze by Maurice Lambert. The ship was full of such artistic gems. (University Archives, University of Liverpool).

ern poster advertising "Ye Olde Fudge Factory and Juice Bar". I make no apology for repeating this latter criticism, for in my view it is symbolic of what has gone wrong in the *Queen Mary*. I have no doubt that the fudge and juice dispensed here are absolutely first class, but there is a place for everything, and the Long Gallery of the greatest ship ever built is not that place. The poignancy of the symbolism is of course that the poster covers a typical English country scene. Need I say more?

But hopefully now we have passed through the Mickey Mouse Spectacular age, and the Queen has survived it, as she survived many other storms in earlier days. Now perhaps we may look forward to her future with renewed hope. Now perhaps is the time for all concerned with her welfare to forget the recent past, to plan for the future, to accentuate the positive. And what a challenge this represents!

To meet this challenge the greatest change of all is required, and that is a change of heart, a realisation that past policies have been wrong and that conservation and profit can go hand in hand and grow together. But first must come the dream, the idea, the inspiration. The Irish poet O'Shaughnessy put it in a nutshell when he wrote -

One man with a dream, at pleasure,
Shall go forth and conquer a crown;
And three with a new song's measure
Can trample an empire down.

Is this too fanciful? Too romantic? Then let me quote Henry Ford again, the most practical of business men and yet a great visionary. He said that in his business he would never record failures for it simply did not follow that because one man had failed in a particular task, another man could not come along and succeed in doing it. Incidentally, he also said he would never be involved in any business that was controlled by accountants. For though the "bottom line" is of vital importance, the figures on a piece of paper should never be permitted to stifle or stem the flow of ideas which are at the heart of every successful undertaking.

So where do we start? Let us start by dreaming a little, by expressing the hope that at long last we are in fact going to witness the rebirth of a Queen, the rekindling of a sincere and genuine interest in the *Queen Mary* as a ship, and especially as a ship with a personality and a soul of her own. Not just a building any more. I was delighted to be a member of the Panel that helped to celebrate the 59th anniversary, and to have the opportunity of saying that I believed that this rebirth was about to happen, that she had a great future, and that her finest hour was yet to come.

How may we assist the rebirth? First and foremost of course by a unity of purpose. Do you remember the parable of the man who had six sons who were always squabbling amongst themselves, and as a consequence never got anywhere? He called them all together and produced six sticks which he said represented the six of them. And he demonstrated that singly he could quite easily break each stick in two, but that if all six sticks were bound together in a bundle it was quite impossible even to bend them.

This is exactly the situation facing the

Above: *Detail from one of the many Main Deck Staterooms, every one of which was different.* (University Archives, University of Liverpool).

Top Right: *Tourist 'A' Deck Lounge Clock and surround by Rebel Stanton.*

Right: *Leaving New York. Battery Park, Manhatten, in the centre, Brooklyn River on the Right.* (University Archives, University of Liverpool).

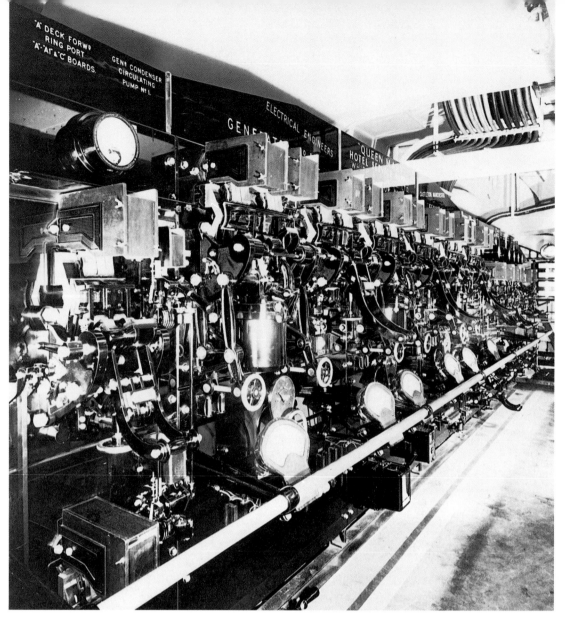

Queen Mary at the present time. There are many hundreds, if not thousands, of people throughout the world who have the welfare of the ship very much at heart, who wish to see her preserved and established as one of the modern wonders of the world. But there are many theories and ideas floating about as to how this may be done, and until these are all collated and bundled together there is always a danger that one idea after another will be tried and discarded, simply because by itself it is not the complete solution.

So what we need is a grand plan of campaign, a statement of objectives in which we can all agree and work towards, a positive policy that will unite us all and inspire us to achieve the seemingly impossible. And it can be done. I am reminded of the Rules of the United Society of Cordwainers, a trade group of leather workers in England in 1799, who concluded their rules with the following inspiring words -

"Let every man lay aside his own private interest and study the good of the whole.

And lastly, let us study friendship and unanimity with one another, this will cement our structure and render it permanent.

Make us the joy of the present and the praise of ages to come."

Who will provide a similar lead to us today? Will it come from the professionals, the management of the ship? Or will it be from the amateurs, the *Queen Mary* Foundation? Or will it ultimately come from the ship's owners, the City of Long Beach, who at the end of the day have most to gain or lose? All that can be said with complete certainty is that to ensure the future of the ship and her continued prosperity and preservtion, an inspirational lead is necessary, and that for this we are all waiting, eager to give what help we can.

Above: *'A ship with personality!* (Diane Rush).
Top Left: *Hotel Services Switchboard, where I spent many hours of watch keeping.* (University Archives, University of Liverpool).
Left: *Difficult to believe, but this is what it looks like now.*

Chapter 10

Positive Possibilities

In a previous chapter (No. 5) I listed one or two of the disappointing changes that have taken place in the *Queen Mary* during her retirement years in Long Beach, and with your permission I should now like to return to some of these and re-examine them. What I would like to do is look at them in a positive way, and see if I, as an interested onlooker, can make any practical suggestions as to what may be done, bearing in mind the constant and overriding need to generate revenue in excess of expenditure.

Let us first look at the Working Alleyway. This was such an important part of the working ship that I have a sneaking suspicion that any general restoration work should begin by restoring the Working Alleyway. This may be extremely difficult, and as a revenue producer it may never be in the top grade, except as an essential and vital part of each and every tour of the ship. Its psychological importance as an essential part of the ship's anatomy cannot be overemphasised, for without it visitors cannot possibly understand how such an enormous and complex organism as an ocean going luxury liner could be run and controlled. It would help to explain how a ship's company of over 3000 souls could be transported at high speed across one of the stormiest oceans in the world, some of them in considerable comfort.

Any restoration of the Working Alleyway

would inevitably I suppose have to be carried out a bit at a time. but I believe that even the announcement that this was to be done would create interest and have a beneficial psychological effect. The publication of a proposed programme of restoration, even if at this stage it could only be an indication of intent, would also help to boost morale and raise spirits.

One more word about the Working Alleyway. Could we please drop this absurd nickname of "the Burma Road" and return to its rightful name? I appreciate the sentimental attraction of a war-time nickname, but Burma Road presents quite the wrong image of the Working Alleyway, and suggests the road to hell.

The next area I would like to reconsider is of course the Promenade Deck which, as mentioned in Chapter 5, was originally one of the most striking features of the ship. At the moment parts of this Deck are revenue producing through the Promenade Cafe and Bar, and the Chelsea Restaurant, and a start has been made in introducing retail trading outlets on other parts of the Deck itself. Unfortunately these retail units obstruct even more of the deck and are something of an architectural eyesore, adding nothing to the ambience of the area.

With respect I would like to suggest that the thinking behind the introduction of retail shops here is very nearly, but not quite, on

The original 3rd Class Entrance Hall. Is this under-utilised at the moment? (University Archives, University of Liverpool).

target. Every small village and town has a High Street, a main shopping street, and it would seem logical for the *Queen Mary* to have one too. And the Promenade Deck, or to be more precise the original first class portion of this deck, would admirably fit the bill. But the shops, and any other retail outlets such as restaurants, should be housed off the deck, in other words inboard of the deck itself, just as in a Main Street on land where nothing of course is built on the street itself. And there is ample room in the *Queen Mary* for this to be done.

What a superb shopping street this would make! A promenade over a quarter of a mile long, and lined with shops and restaurants. Would it be worth the upheaval and cost that would inevitably have to be borne? Cost would obviously be high, and only a feasibility study would decide the issue. Relocation of the Promenade Cafe and Chelsea Restaurant would be necessary, but with the present low utilisation of space at Promenade Deck level this should not be impossible.

There are several areas on this deck that would benefit from a utilisation study anyway, irrespective of what long term plan is adopted, as for example the area that origi-

nally contained the Long Gallery, Ballroom, Starboard Gallery and the First Class Smoking Room. As mentioned before, the loss of some of these elegant public rooms is much to be regretted, and in any plans for restoration these areas provide much scope.

Another part of the ship that qualifies for consideration, and in my view is sending out piteous cries for help is the old Verandah Grill. To anyone who remembers the elegance, sophistication and intimate character of this delightful little grill room its present condition is most hurtful. In the *Queen Mary*'s early years in Long Beach it was only natural for her new owners to explore every catering possibility, for without some

No sea views from this room, but it would make a magnificent restaurant. (University Archives, University of Liverpool).

experimentation it would have been extremely difficult to decide which section of the market would produce the best return. So perhaps they can be forgiven for deciding to cover the whole range from fast food up to the most sophisticated.

What seems so regrettable is the unhappy choice of the Verandah Grill to supply the bottom end of the market, and I just wonder if it would not repay to rethink this area and consider integrating the Verandah Grill into the Sir Winston's complex. If the Burger Bar end of the market is so profitable that it would be foolish to give it up, could it not be transferred to the other end of the ship, to the old Third Class area which is lamentably under-utilised at present? It has been suggested that consideration should be given to providing some sort of late night Snack Bar or Coffee Shop in part of the old Third Class accommodation, and it could well be worth while studying this possibility in depth.

Another suggestion that has been put forward is the possible provision of facilities for young people in the forward part of the ship. This sounds like a very profitable area for investigation, for obviously it is important to attract young people to the ship for they are the citizens of tomorrow. I must confess at being ignorant of what existing facilities there are for young people in Long Beach, but I suspect that in common with the rest of the civilised world there is a size-

able Youth problem. Anything that can be done to help young people to a healthy way of life, and steer them away from the many evils of this world is much to be applauded.

The hotel and catering facilities at present available in the *Queen Mary* presumably account for much of her profitability, and if this is so one is immediately struck by the fact that these operations occupy only the top five of her twelve decks. So what about the other seven? How can they be more fully utilised and brought into profit bearing? Surely the vast spaces down below once occupied by the boiler and engine rooms can be used to provide attractions both to the tourist and the business man, as well as to the historian.

Many excellent ideas for new and exciting tours of the ship have already been put forward, and this is obviously a step in the right direction, for the more people you can

Once the most elegant room in the ship. Just the spot for a Burger Bar? (University Archives, University of Liverpool).

Above: *Entrance to Sir Winston's, now the most elegant restaurant in the ship, built on top of a Burger Bar!*

Below: *Is it possible? This was Boiler Room No.4.*

encourage to come aboard the better. So the problem basically is to find more and more interesting things for them to see and do, and as her life as a ship has never been fully exploited, the scope is enormous. Several suggestions present themselves and some of these are listed below, though not necessarily in the order in which it would be possible to adopt them.

All visitors, I believe, would have been interested to see her original propulsion machinery, and the present remnant that has been preserved in the After Engine Room does not give anything like a true impression of what it was like down below in 1936. Obviously this cannot now be reproduced, but I believe a very fair facsimile of certain parts of it, and of the general layout, could be, and indeed should be, recreated.

What I have in mind is the very fascinating walk that it was possible to take from end to end of the vessel's machinery spaces, for this walk covered the whole process of raising steam and generating the electricity that were necessary to power the main engines, and indeed to provide life for the whole of the ship.

Starting up forward in No. 1 Boiler Room you would see the three Scotch Boilers that provided steam for the Hotel Services Generating Station turbines, and from here you would pass through an Air Lock into Boiler Room No. 2. Down the centre of this Boiler Room you could walk and through another Air Lock into the Forward or Hotel Services Generating Room. Through here and into another Air Lock leading to Boiler Room No. 3, and thence into Boiler Room No. 4. Each Boiler Room was of course entered and left by an Air Lock since Nos. 2 to 5 were all operated at a slightly higher air pressure than atmospheric, as described in Chapter 2.

From Boiler Room No. 4 you would pass into the Main Machinery Generating Room, the slightly larger of the two Power Stations, and thence into the last of the Boiler Rooms, No. 5. The exit from No. 5 would take you straight into the Forward Engine Room which visually was quite different to the After one, the reason for this being that the two forward engines drive the outer screws and the two after engines drive the inner screws. This means that in the Forward Engine Room the Condensers, which are by far the bulkiest part of the engine, have to be situated in the centre of the engine room with the turbines and propeller shafts outboard of them, and in the After Engine Room the arrangement is reversed. It follows therefore that the Starting Platform in the After Engine Room, which is in the centre, is much more open and spacious looking than the Starting Platform of the Forward Engine Room, and is hence more impressive to look at, but it must be remembered that functionally the two engine rooms are identical.

From the Forward Engine Room, in which of course the air is at atmospheric pressure, you pass into the After Engine Room, and from thence into the Shaft Tunnels (not, please, Shaft *Alleyways* as they have subsequently been dubbed.) The total length of the walk I have described is possibly not much more than 600 feet, but it took you past some of the finest marine engineering equipment ever built, equipment capable of producing almost 200,000 Horse Power, powerful enough to drive this mammoth vessel for several days on end at over 30 knots.

Unfortunately this is now gone and is unlikely every to be reproduced, but such is the skill of the model makers art these days that I believe parts of it could be simulated to give visitors a very real insight as to what it was like.

I believe it would be possible, for example, to create, at reasonable cost, a walk through a typical boiler room, with authentic temperatures, noises and smells, to build an authentic looking air lock which visitors could pass through, and even to show them what the two generating stations looked like.

In this connection I would like to tell you of an experience I had many years ago. The company I worked for after leaving the *Queen Mary* manufactured crucibles and electric furnaces for melting non-ferrous metals. An English film company came and asked for advice as they wanted to simulate a foundry in which gold was being melted. We ended up lending them a furnace and they installed this on the set and alongside it built an identical one in plywood. This second one was so faithful a copy that even standing alongside it you had difficulty in detecting which one was real and which one false. The film they were making was "The Lavender Hill Mob" which some of you may have seen.

This collaboration incidentally developed

and ripened, and led to many visits to the film studios where I could not but marvel at the brilliant way in which they were deceiving the public with their art. In one subsequent film they even invaded our Works and shot several scenes there. In the studio they reconstructed parts of our factory and offices with uncanny accuracy, and I firmly believe now that any building, street, or machine can be effectively reproduced. For the record this second film was "The Man In The White Suit" starring Alec Guiness, Cecil Parker and Joan Greenwood, and when these stars were in the factory hundreds of autograph books appeared as if by magic. Production (of our products) was not too good while all this was going on.

I believe such a tour as I have suggested would be immensely popular and would earn money, and am tempted to go even further. Where a watertight bulkhead was situated, as for example between boiler rooms, a watertight door occurred inside the air lock. These doors were hydraulically operated and were normally kept open, but in the event of fog or any other dangerous condition they were immediately shut, being automatically operated from the bridge, their shutting being preceded by the clanging of very loud bells.

Each door could be opened individually to enable engineers to pass through the bulkhead by operating a handle, but the door closed automatically as soon as the handle was released.

For the adventurous visitor it would be possible to create an air lock containing a watertight door, the procedure for passing through being to enter the air lock, closing the door behind you, then opening the watertight door and passing through before the door has time to shut, and then letting yourself out at the other side. This may sound dangerous, but was not really so, and there is no reason why the mock watertight door should be heavy enough to hurt anybody who might get trapped. These watertight doors of course opened horizontally or sideways, but the one between the two engine rooms was a vertical one. This one was much more interesting for it opened upwards, and started to descend like a guillotine as soon as you let got of the operating lever. It was not advisable to loiter as you passed through this door!

In the next chapter I propose to suggest one or two other ideas that might be adopted to attract visitors, ideas which have been well tried in other places, and found to be successful.

WOW!
— THERE'S RON WINTER!!

Chapter 11

What Next?

A hundred years ago or more in England, long before the days of movies, radio, or television as a principal source of entertainment, the Victorians developed a form of amusement which for a time became very popular. This consisted of small groups of actors and actresses posing on a stage and recreating well known scenes from history, the object being to compose a still picture that had the merit of being either beautiful, interesting, or humorous. To give this form of entertainment a little class (with a capital K) they gave it a French title - *Tableaux Vivants*.

Today this would seem to us to be a pretty gloomy form of entertainment, and as an art form it did not have a very long life, but it developed in several directions. One of these was in the form of waxworks which rapidly became fashionable, and which indeed still retain their popularity today. Perhaps one of the best known and thriving waxworks is Madame Tussauds in London in which you can see figures of well known statesmen, politicians, royalty, criminals, film stars, etc. and little scenes from world history. Technology has improved to such an extent since the early days of waxworks that it is virtually impossible to distinguish the wax figures from the real thing, and many people have been deceived (by both).

Another way in which the *Tableaux Vivants* idea developed was in the Minsky Burlesque type of entertainment, which staged immobile scenes of nudity, the law for a time permitting nude figures on stage providing it was motionless. Today we seem to have got over this form of prudery which

many people nowadays find rather quaint.

The waxworks idea has been developed a stage further in that a continuous story can now be told, by linking together a number of tableaux, and by the addition of subtle lighting effects, a spoken commentary, and a musical background, a very realistic effect can be produced.

Such an entertainment can currently be seen in Canterbury, Kent, in England where "The Canterbury Tales" are enacted in an old redundant church which has been converted for the purpose. This is the story of a band of pilgrims in the Middle Ages travelling from Southwark in London to worship at the shrine of St. Thomas a'Becket, the Archbishop who in 1170 was murdered in Canterbury Cathedral. In this show the visitor walks through a series of authentic medieval

rooms depicting various places the pilgrims passed through, and in each of these is portrayed the events that took place there. Lighting, sound, and realistic figures dressed in authentic medieval costumes play a big part in the effectiveness of this show which attracts a continuous stream of visitors during the season.

There are many shows of this type in England, and I have no doubt in America too, and all of them are money spinners, for when done professionally they are extremely effective. In my view some of the great empty spaces of the *Queen Mary*'s boiler rooms would lend themselves admirably to this type of entertainment, and there would be no problem in choosing a number of interesting scenes in the life of the ship in her sailing days. For example, a series of scenes could cover a typical voyage from New York to Southampton, or the Maiden Voyage from Southampton to New York. Others could depict scenes aboard in fine weather contrasted with those in rough weather, and it would bring home to visitors what rolling was really like to construct a room tilted to over 40 degrees! War time scenes could also be shown and even, for those who like horror stories, the accident with *H.M.S.Curacoa*. The list is a very long one and judging from the popularity of similar land based entertainments it could prove to be a crowd puller.

If this type of show were adopted there is now on the market another development which would increase its effectiveness even more. This is marketed in England under the name of "Talking Heads" and is uncannily realistic. It consists of producing some of the human figures used in these tableaux complete in every detail with the exception of their faces which are left flat and blank. Facial expressions and features are then supplied by means of a film projector, and the result is quite startling, the figure apparently coming to life. A figure by this means could talk to the onlooker, looking him straight in the eye, or two figures could have a conversation, the deception practised being very convincing.

There is no doubt that a moving exhibit is far more attractive than a stationary one, and experience of mounting exhibitions of comparatively unglamorous engineering products taught me that two things will stop the average visitor in his tracks - a moving exhibit or a pretty girl. There is room for the use of both of them in advertising the *Queen Mary*. In considering the use of "Talking Heads" what about scenes from American history, or for that matter even British history? I cannot imagine anything more dramatic than a Talking Head of Abraham Lincoln delivering the Gettysburg Address!

Another 'live' activity which always attracts interest, and one that is already being used in the *Queen Mary*, is to have a model maker at work. Human nature is such that it is always fascinating to watch someone else working, and I just wonder if this idea could not be developed and expanded to have several craft activities carried on, making souvenirs of the ship for sale. Small wooden models of the *Queen Mary* would surely sell, and it would also be worth considering the establishment of a small craft pottery or even glassworks making articles bearing the ship's name.

No reference to models would be complete without mentioning the 22 foot scale model of the complete ship as she was in 1936 now nearing completion by Robin B. Jacobs. A sample of Mr. Jacob's art is already on display in the ship's Exhibition Hall, this being a working model of one of the 24 Yarrow water tube boilers. The model of the whole ship is being built to the same high standard, and when completed it should surely prove to be a compelling exhibit. Alternatively, if parts of the model's machinery could be seen in operation a great interest would be created.

Having written about the importance of moving exhibits to attract attention it may seem like an anti-climax to revert to a static

Above: *A passenger alleyway in 1936. There were two per deck on Main, 'A' and 'B' decks.* (University Archives, University of Liverpool).

Below: *A passenger alleyway in 1993.*

Among the finest art treasures in the ship were paintings on white hide in the Tourist Main Lounge by Margot Gilbert. They represented dancing throughout the world and were exquisite.
(University Archives, University of Liverpool).

Above: *Alas all that is left now. Being examined by a bemused Julian Hill (in background), Robin Jacobs, Dick Backus, Pat Winter, Ron Winter, Ron Smith, and Maria DuBry.*

Right: *Even one of the remaining fragments has been vandalised.*

museum, but obviously there is a need for this as well. The current *Queen Mary* Exhibition is interesting and informative and I believe is constantly under review with a view to enlargement and improvement. To the visitor, and particularly to one with no knowledge of maritime matters and ship design, it is necessary for the *Queen Mary* story to be spelled out stage by stage, each phase of her life - design, construction, operation, war service, rehabilitation, and retirement - being dealt with clearly and systematically. If this is done then the interest of the visitor will not only be maintained but enhanced, and at the end of the exhibition he should then have to exit through the souvenir shop, and past a desk where he should be encouraged to join the *Queen Mary* Foundation.

It should not be necessary for me to emphasise that this last suggestion presupposes that the *Queen Mary* Foundation and the professional management of the ship are working together as a team, with the same object in view, namely the preservation, glorification, and economic viability of this great ship. As an amateur organisation of enthusiasts the *Queen Mary* Foundation has much to offer, and the individual skills of its members should be fully utilised in service to the ship. Personally, I would like to see amateur labour used to help organise and augment the following -

1. An Archives Department that covered not only the *Queen Mary* but also a history of Transatlantic Ferries from 1840 to the present day. Including of course a list of all Transatlantic liners.
2. A Reference Library of all books about transatlantic travel.
3. A world-wide Research Facility in conjunction with the above to keep in contact with other archival collections both in America and Europe.
4. Cataloguing all original fittings and furniture, etc. still extant in the ship. Separating the genuine from the fake. Tracing the whereabouts of art treasures that have gone astray, etc.
5. The restoration of original furniture in need of repair, some of which could be valuable.
6. Helping as tour guides.

There are many ways in which the enthusiasm and skills of Foundation members can be harnessed and made to work for the good of the ship, and there is nothing like participation in a worthwhile project for creating a successful and happy ambience.

In concluding this chapter on what to do next I would like to emphasise that the sole object has been to mention some of the ideas that occur to me as an interested visitor, and to repeat Henry Ford's dictum that you should never write off a failed idea. If you try it again it might work!

Other opinions

It has been my good fortune to meet a great many people, both in Britain and America, who have an abiding love for the *Queen Mary* and a sincere wish to see her preserved. In Britain we say surely if we can preserve *H.M.S. Warrior,* an early 19th century ship, the *Cutty Sark,* greatest of the Clipper ships, and Nelson's *Victory,* the ultimate example built in the 18th century, then surely we can preserve the *Queen Mary*, a 20th century ship and an absolute youngster compared to any of the above. The very idea of her being scrapped, or sold off for some ignoble purpose, is abhorrent.

My own experience in talking to people, both individually and collectively, about the ship is that there is an overwhelming feeling that she should be preserved at all costs. My experience covers talking to groups of all sorts of people, both male and female, from those who have a specialised knowledge of nautical affairs, to those who do not know

one end of a ship from the other, and the total addressed now numbers many thousands. Of those who not only love ships and the sea, but also have a particular affection for the *Queen Mary*, there are many whom I am happy and proud to call my friends, and I have asked several of these to contribute to this book by giving us all the benefit and pleasure of their opinions and feelings about the ship.

The response to this appeal has been heartwarming, to say the least, and I am delighted to devote the next few chapters to those "Other Opinions". The contributors come from all walks of life, and each has an individual point of view. I have written a short introduction to each one, just to remind you, the reader, of the particular qualifications of the writer, and I am sure you will agree that their contributions demonstrate very clearly that the affection for this ship is literally world-wide.

Chapter 12

That Wonderful Ship
by George Kean

George Kean is a typical Scot, and more particularly he is a Shipwright and a typical "Bankie", as natives of Clydebank are affectionately known. In other words he is hard working, sincere, and dependable, the type that once made Britain Great. George is at heart a poet, and though not given to unnecessary speech, what he does say, or write, is always worth noting.

I was just fourteen years of age when I first became aware of the wonderful ship. My Dad, who was a shipyard riveter, said it was to be the largest ship in the world and it would provide work for many Bankies for two or three years. Clydebank was very dependent on the success of the Singer Sewing Machine Company and John Brown's Shipyard at that time, and whole families were employed in both companies. I had left school early because I was working in Jardine's Barber Shop, just outside the shipyard gate. I got to know all the foremen and workers. My family consisted of three older brothers and one younger brother, and my Mum was always saying "Five boys, and no one to do the washing up."

Work began on No. 534 in December 1930. No name was mentioned for the ship. Work became plentiful, the depression was fading. Families began to recover from the bleak days of the depression in Clydebank and Glasgow. 534 became a symbol of recovery. We had emerged from a bad dream. One of my favourite customers was Mr. William McKenzie who was the shipyard Welfare Officer. He promised to find me a job when I became fifteen. Barber shop wages were only five shillings, but my tips more than made up for that.

All went smoothly until the end of the following year, then disaster struck. The newspaper headlines spelt it out. "Work on 534 to stop. Cunard have run out of cash and the Government are unable to help." Mass unemployment was back with us again. But Mr. McKenzie did not forget his promise. He arranged for me to start work in the West Yard where two destroyers were being built, and when I was sixteen I would begin my apprenticeship to become a Shipwright.

I entered the yard gate and made my way to where I had to work, and on the way I had to pass the huge silent hull of 534 and I wondered when it would ever be completed. Every dinner hour I would sit by the gangway of 534 and imagine myself walking up with my tools to begin work on the largest liner in the world. I had been put in the charge of a Loftsman Shipwright to learn my trade. Allen Adam was a Christian gentleman, he was strict but fair, and would slap my face if I said 'damn'. He taught me well.

After about ten months Mr. Adam was called to head office and when he returned he was very excited. He said "George, your dream has come true. No. 534 is to be restarted and we are going aboard her to remove all the dead-lights from the portholes and let the daylight in." I was in heaven as we walked up the wooden gangway to 'A' Deck. As we walked there was no sound of our footsteps. It was so eerie, a carpet of thick dust had gathered in the two years of inactivity.

Very soon the ship became a hubbub of noise and hearty laughter as everyone gathered outside the gates for the great return to work. There were pipe bands playing, church bells ringing from Glasgow to Clydebank, and not a sad face in sight. It was such a wonderful 534 feeling. Can you wonder why 534 was such a godsend to us? And has stayed in our minds for so long? 534 was truly a wonderful ship even before she entered the River Clyde as R.M.S. *Queen Mary*.

The liner was duly launched on 26th September with a full spring tide, and it poured with rain all through the proceedings. I think that God was providing as much water as possible for her journey to her natural environment. I was under the ship that day to help remove strategic blocks at intervals until the last moment, but she was so anxious to get to the water we had to abandon the last six blocks and make a dash for safety as she slid down the ways and entered the water. We were just in time to hear the Queen christen her R.M.S. *Queen Mary*.

Sixteen years ago an American gentleman named Hal Johnson visited the Yard which was now taken over by Marathon U.K. Ltd., who were building oil rigs - and I was their Safety Manager. So because of my association with the liner I took charge of him. Hal and I had a wonderful day walking up and down the original berth. Hal could hardly

believe that such a large liner had been launched into such a small river. Hal told me he was a diver and looked after the Queen's posterior. He said the ship was in wonderful condition and was called Hyatt Hotels. He made me promise to write to the franchise owners, which I have done ever since when finally Long Beach City Council took over the job.

About a year ago a young Californian lady named Diane Rush, who had fallen in love with the great ship, contacted me to ask if I would like to visit the Queen for the 59th birthday celebrations. I thought it was too good to be true, but I did make the journey along with celebrities from Clydebank. Diane, who is Director of the *Queen Mary* Foundation, and I finally stood on the teakwood decks which I had helped to lay so many years ago. I looked at Diane's triumphant, glowing face and was so grateful for all the work she and her friends had accomplished. I felt as if I was home.

I would like to see the great ship made secure for posterity. It is almost a legend now and I am sure it will go down in history as the ship with a soul. The ship that shortened the second world war by out-speeding the might of Hitler's navy, so much so that he put a price on her head. It is good to know that 534 is in good hands in Long Beach, California. I used to sing "God Save the Queen" until I got to Long Beach and found that it was Joseph Prevratil who actually saved the Queen.

Finally, how did we get there? Well, an angel called Lisa Lynn Backus carried us through the air, without even a bump.

Chapter 13

The Royal Progress
by Hal Johnson

There is more to Hal Johnson than might appear at first sight. Underneath his bluff exterior and behind his undoubted technical qualifications as a diver and surveyor lurks a very sensitive and caring human being. His shattering experience in the Korean War had a profound effect on him, and sharpened up his gift for writing satirical prose, but his affection for the Queen Mary shines through and is an example to all of us.
The following article covers four stages in the life of the Queen, and was first printed in the Avalon Bay News.

3rd April 1934, Clydebank, Scotland
One April morning in 1934 the news came that the British Government had provided the Cunard Line with a loan for Clydebank's shipbuilders to finish the *Queen Mary*'s construction. Less than a week later, the day that had so long been prayed for at last arrived. In the darkness of the predawn hours, several hundred men had gathered around the shipyard's main entrance. The first light of day found most of them so anxious to get back to work that they couldn't wait for their shift to begin. They invaded the yard and began climbing up to their respective job sites.

That still and silent gigantic steel frame was swiftly coming alive with the vigorous activity of proud men eager to do what they did best, build ships.

Long columns of workers were walking out onto dust laden scaffolds and steel frames. Beneath their tread, the ghostly fall of time's forgotten residue caught the gathering light of the sunrise over the River Clyde. Within the passage of early sunlight through all of that elaborate framework, clouds of glittering dust particles drifted down and all about the *Queen Mary*'s colossal skeleton.

Though the work had already begun, the shipyard horns blasted out their call for the day shift to commence. The raucous signal of those blaring horns became lost in the resounding roar of over a thousand joyously cheering workmen. In response to those thunderous cries, the church bells from Clydebank to Glasgow rang out all up and down the Clyde. Amid the tumult, the *Queen Mary*'s structural frame came full aglow in the shimmering iridescence of a golden dawn.

The largest and fastest ocean liner that had ever been built arose out of the darkest descents into poverty ever known to the Western World's modern history. From those times' indomitable strivings for human dignity, a great ship sailed forth into all that man and sea could pit against her. During war and peace, this world's supremely reigning trans-oceanic monarch seaworthily responded to all that the free world could possibly ask of her.

1993 Southern California is a long time and far away from those Scottish lowland scenes of the *Queen Mary*'s impoverished yet inspiring origins. However great the distance between those uncertain times and these, who can credibly claim that this magnificent old vessel has lost any of her first-found graces of power to evoke the euphoria of her jubilantly returning workers?

Moreover, whenever the silhouette of the Atlantic Queen is being vividly defined by one of the Pacific's blazing sunsets, is Her Maritime Majesty's twilight place in time any less aglow with faith restoring brilliance than it was on that momentous April dawn of 1934?

12th May 1979, Clydebank, Scotland

"Why on earth did you come to Clydebank for a vacation?" This was the question that was asked me by a completely bewildered office secretary. She could not understand how I could possibly find pleasure in her place of daily toil, the executive offices of what was once John Brown's Shipyard.

My answer to that lady's question seemed to further convince her that I should be brought before proper authorities and officially declared mentally incompetent.

"Regardless of how dismally these river banks may be perceived," I contended, "there are certain feelings about their history that deserve to be warmly cherished. Such fond feelings fill the heart of any man or woman whose life has ever been graced by one or more of the great ships that were constructed here. The most magnificent of these vessels was, of course, the *Queen Mary*. As Her Maritime Majesty's maintenance and inspection diver, all my gropings beneath her waterline have left me with a solemn debt of gratitude to Clydebank's shipbuilders. I have travelled from California in order to see where Her Highness was built and launched. Is this too much to expect for a guy who has become more familiar with the Queen's bottom than any other man in living history."

My expressions of ardour for Her Maritime Majesty's huge posterior proceeded with ever increasing passion. These passions were about to reach their peak when the lady before me cried into an office intercom system. "George, this is Lilly. Please come to the outer office immediately."

As George Kean entered, Lilly told him that I should quickly be taken out of her office for a tour of what remains of John Brown's Shipyard. Lilly's voice had grown somewhat shrill and tremulous as she repeated her request that the proposed tour begin as soon as possible.

30th September 1992, Long Beach, California

The *Queen Mary*'s rescue from the international auction block leaves far more to be celebrated than realised. The sale of the Queen to that auction's highest bidder would have left her to be towed across the Pacific to Hong Kong. In all likelihood she would have remained moored in that city's harbor beyond Mainland China's 1997 scheduled reclamation of this territory's jurisdiction.

The marxist state that would have ultimately become heir to this vessel is already heir to a far more lucrative enterprise. Communist China is enjoying an ever-growing fortune from its arms manufacture and sales business with terrorists and Third World demagogues. In keeping with this enterprise, Red China's heavy investments in armed conquest and ideological conversion has cornered the markets of North Korea, South East Asia, Tibet, Burma, and its own people.

Recent European and Japanese capitalisations upon Asia's marxist revolutionary commerce almost included Long Beach, California's take of 20.1 million dollars for the *Queen Mary*.

Though it was a British concern which would have initially acquired the Queen, her moorings in Hong Kong Harbor would have doubtlessly remained intact long after mainland China's re-established claim to that city.

The Korean War's military conscription of this writer leaves me sadly lacking in that level of sophistication which is able to forget the way that a certain militarily conscripted passenger ship served during World War II. Throughout the time I was an eleven to fifteen year old Long Beach schoolboy, the *Queen Mary* was vigorously criss-crossing the Nazi submarine infested North Atlantic. Carrying up to sixteen thousand troops per voyage left her prey to one of the most exhaustive search-and-destroy campaigns in the history of modern warfare. As the Queen's thirty-three knot speed eluded all that the German Navy could hurl at her, this ocean line became the pride of the Clydebank, Scotland, shipyard that built her.

All of those pre-World War II accommodations of Adolf Hitler's and Hiro Hito's war machines were as myopically pre-occupied with fiscal security and gain as those of contemporary Long Beach ambitions to profitably unload the *Queen Mary* in Hong Kong Harbor. If these ambitions would have had their way, Long Beach would have eventually been geopolitically recognised for its expertise in a specific field of mercantile endeavour. Such expertise rules from both marxism's and capitalism's highest and lowest places that "Anything is for sale to anyone, anywhere, any time, as long as the price is right and the seller is immune to the long-range mortal and financial consequences of such commerce".

No one can doubt the historical implications of any part of a democracy which would, for the first price, surrender to tyranny a great ship which was once heroically instrumental in the defeat of tyranny.

As a credit to the powers of the democratic process to keep the peace, Long Beach's duly elected local government voted seven to two in favour of preserving the *Queen Mary*'s reign over this city's waterfront. The political concept of a self-governing people has thusly triumphed over that profound knowledge of the price of everything and the value of nothing.

23rd September 1993,
Long Beach, California

George Kean and his wife Betty, arrived aboard the *Queen Mary*. They are part of an entourage of festively fun-loving yet attentively curious Britons. Certain members of this hardy group had played vital roles in Her Maritime Majesty's design, construction, and transatlantic voyages. The occasion of their visit is the 59th anniversary of the Queen's launching.

As a lad of sixteen years, George Kean had begun his career as an apprentice shipwright in 1934. His first project consisted of fitting and fastening the *Queen Mary*'s teak decks. Until this trip to Long Beach, George had not seen Her Highness since she was towed down the Clyde in 1936.

This life-long builder of great ships was asked many questions during his Long Beach visit. The bare-bones brevity of his quick responses represents one of rhetoric's most endangered species. There was, for example, George's response to a question which was asked by Gordon Dillow, a Los Angeles Times journalist. Mr. Dillow inquired, "Is it true that the *Queen Mary* has over three million rivets in her hull?" Mr. Kean answered, "I don't know. I never counted them."

Among these poignant jewels was one which was solicited by Lisa Lynn Backus, the chief promoter and organiser of this British visit aboard the Queen. Lisa asked George "Have you ever seen anything to confirm all those reports that the *Queen Mary* is haunted by several ghosts from her illustrious past?" George replied, "No, I don't drink."

George and I had become good friends the day that he heroically rescued Lilly from the mad clutches of this ardent caretaker of Her Maritime Majesty's bottom. I therefore took the liberty of attempting to transform George's lean cuts of precise English beef into a verbally chaotic stampede. This rhetorical rout was attempted while my old Scottish buddy was being photographed amid a large crowd of his adoring fans. At the moment the photographer was focusing his camera, I falsely informed George that he had left the fly of his pants open.

Though George hears as well as he wants to hear, he kept insisting that he could not understand what I was softly saying to him. This 76 year old retired shipbuilder would not be content until he had baited me into shouting, "Your fly is open, George." At that point he had the stage set for the longest speech of his oratory career.

"This," George proclaimed, "Is not a fly. It's an eagle!"

Britain is indeed Great.

God save the Queen!

Chapter 14

Lasting Memories from an
Island Childhood

by David F. Hutchings

The name of David Hutchings is well known throughout the world wherever the Queen Mary is discussed, for his books about the ship have had wide acclaim. David was born and educated in the Isle of Wight where daily he saw all the great liners passing by.

Read now the fascinating story of his love affair with the greatest of them all.

"*Queen Mary*" - the very words conjure images of monarchy, luxury and exclusiveness. Indeed, the great liner that still bears that regal appellation embodied all these qualities and, for many breathtakingly wonderful years, ruled as the undisputed Queen of the Atlantic. She transported the rich and the famous in the cosseted sanctuary of her first class accommodation and, for the other classes, in a luxury that had barely been imagined a few years previously.

Few ships have ever equalled the impact that the *Queen Mary* made when she was built, launched and commissioned in the 1930's, and such is the impression that the ship has had since her launch sixty years ago that the vessel has often been regarded as the epitome of the ocean liner. When talk is of the Western Ocean and the myriad of ships that have crossed its often tortuous tracks, the peacetime and wartime exploits of the Queen makes an important contribution to the discussion.

My own love of this great liner began when, as a school boy who had been born and bred in the village of Gurnard (near Cowes) on the Isle of Wight, I became used

to the commonplace sight of the world's greatest liners passing - practically daily - through the confines of the Solent on their way to and from Southampton, an occurrence that became taken for granted.

By the time that I was about seven I started taking a perfunctory interest in the ships that I saw as the talk between my parents and relatives would often revolve around the big yachts and liners that they in turn had been used to before the war. They had even visited liners such as the *Homeric* and *Majestic* whilst berthed in dock at Southampton, paying one shilling (5p) for the privilege.

Eleven years of age found me at school in Cowes with an every growing interest in the liners, especially as many of the passing ships could be seen through the trees from various classrooms. (This interest soon developed to include the predecessors of the vessels that I saw). A list of Solent shipping movements, published weekly in 'The Isle of Wight County Press' would be kept in my desk, along with a much used and treasured copy of the 'Dumpy Book of Ships', to be closely scrutinised each day for the sailing of an old favourite or of a new addition. Invariably, except during their lay-up periods, one of the mighty Queens of the Cunard Line would make a weekly appearance. If a glance was sneaked through the classroom window to see if the expected ship was in sight, an authoritarian voice would boom from the front of the classroom "Pay attention to the blackboard! It's only the *Queen Mary*!" Only!!

If an evening arrival or departure was involved then a break from homework and a four-minute walk would find me on the local beach. I loved to see these ships at night, the Queens in particular and the *'Mary'* most of all. On a quiet, summery Solent evening with only the small flames from Fawley Oil Refinery burning six miles distant, an occasional light showing on the mainland, a rush of stars overhead, a black sea rippling and gently lapping in front of me, and a bell on a channel marker buoy tolling at regular intervals, the sight of the *Queen Mary* inward bound and emerging from behind a not-too-distant headland never ceased to thrill.

First, the bow and foc'sle appeared, its blackness blotting out the lights and glow of the distant Gosport shores replacing them with a few of the ship's own lights picked out in lines that followed the gentle sheer of her hull. Then the higher, looming bridge burst into view with its single red navigation light burning brightly amongst the other pre-neon lights that illuminated the beginning of the white superstructure. Quickly there followed the first of those three incredible funnels, the orange of the floodlit base intensifying into that glorious Cunard red, the black bands defined, picked out in light and shadow, a wisp of grey smoke, made incandescent by the flood of illumination from below, hurriedly exuded from the funnels before disappearing into the following darkness.

Row on row of lights quickly emerged, those on the hull appearing as tiny individual dots whilst the larger ones on the white superstructure blended into one shimmering whole. Soon the ship presented a complete sparkling profile, a silent moving jewel, her reflected light coming towards me on the sea in jagged moving zig-zags of yellow. The feeling of elation that had gripped me gradually diminished as the ship turned to starboard as she followed the channel that led to the entrance of Southampton Water. My imagination was full of the scenes on board, of the music, the excitement, or the relieved resignation of the passengers as they neared their journeys end, and of the interiors of the ship that I had gleaned from my collected brochures.

The Queen continued to make her turn, her lights condensing as she foreshortened prior to making a second turn, this time to port, to bring her head round Calshot Spit Light Vessel towards Southampton. By now I had to remember to step a distance back from the water's edge as the first of a dozen or so heavy breakers, caused by the ship's wash, crashed on to the shingle, dragging stones and seaweed hissingly back between each wave. (The wash of passing ships often caught seasonal holiday makers unawares because of its suddenness - in spite of warnings from the 'locals').

The liner now completed her turn and gradually her lower hull became obscured by Calshot Spit. A few minutes more and even her upperworks disappeared behind the trees of the New Forest, leaving but a glow in the sky above the dark treeline to mark her progress.

Nearby Cowes provided one of the best platforms from which to see passing liners and the then smallish oil tankers lying at anchor as they awaited a berth at Fawley. The holiday season of the summer months always drew large numbers of enthusiastic sightseers who, arriving in coach loads from the various resorts on the Island, waited patiently for one of the stately Queens to make an appearance which would last for a good thirty minutes. Lit by the sun that shone from behind the viewers' backs the liners were always seen to their best advantage and many postcards were produced, some of the best showing the *'Mary'* passing by the gun platform of Cowes Castle, the venerable home of the Royal Yacht Squadron.

A walk home from school along the mile and a half Prince's Esplanade between Cowes and Gurnard occasionally provided a rich harvest for the memory. One such gem had the *'Mary'* inward bound on a late Spring afternoon. As she steamed through Cowes Roads to begin her turn the lowering sun caught her port side, gilding each rivet head in an individual splash of light.

A lunchtime walk down to the Prince's Green also sometimes produced a lasting memory. One day the *'Mary'* was due but because of a thick impenetrable fog, her wonderful, booming siren indicated that she was stationary off Cowes, obviously brought to a halt by the murk. The fog lasted overnight and well into the next day, and a similar walk the next day saw the fog lifting. The *'Mary'* was revealed anchored in all her glory and in company with the Greek Line's *Arkadia*. The latter was still there when the *'Mary'* sailed (if memory serves) the next day after a quick turnround in Southampton. An enterprising photographer, apparently similarly impressed by the scene, recorded the occasion, and his photograph would later be produced as yet another postcard.

Perhaps twice a year, a day trip to Southampton, (usually on a Saturday) would be made in company with my lifelong friend Dick de Kerbrech, also from Gurnard, to snap the in-port liners with our primitive cameras. Seven shillings (35p) would buy a return ticket on either of Red Funnel steamers *Vecta, Balmoral,* or *Medina*. Dock passes could be obtained in Canute Road as could up to date brochures from the various shipping company offices located in the same street. Then the day would be ours to be spent around the docks and walking up and down the quayside with the *Queen Mary* alongside in the Ocean Dock as lorries, vans, cars, trains, etc., arrived or departed with cargoes, supplies, flowers or passengers.

A walk along the balcony of the Ocean Terminal building brought us almost level with the liner's boat deck. Who thought in those far off days that I would eventually meet some of her captains who were then regarded as the equivalent of a Concorde pilot today? In the 1950's they had perhaps the most glamorous jobs in the world.

If a ship was sailing during the time of our visit then a special harbour trip in one of Blue Funnel's pleasure launches put another necessary strain on our limited resources.

When I left school I had to 'emigrate' to the mainland to find employment and my interest in passenger ships unhappily waned. I regretted missing the all too frequent final departures of many of my old favourites in the mid-sixties but in 1967 I did see the *'Mary'* make her last arrival in Southampton from New York when thousands of a similar mind watched in silence as she berthed in a decreasing drizzle. A few weeks later I hoped to see her leave Southampton for the

last time as she sailed for Long Beach but because of various delays, all I saw was the anchor formation helicopter fly past, a group of people standing on the roof of Owen and Owen's store, and heard the distant roar of those beautiful whistles.

Since then my interest in ocean lines has happily been re-kindled with the mighty *Queen Mary* very much to the fore. The time came, too, when I wanted to give back some of the pleasure I had derived from these magnificent creations of man, and it was then I started to write. My first solo book was, of course, about *Queen Mary*, commissioned to celebrate the 50th anniversary of her maiden voyage.

Research and interviews brought me into contact with many people of whom I had heard, but never thought that I would meet, such as Captains Donald MacLean, Geoffrey Marr and John Treasure Jones as well as chefs, stewards, engineers, bell boys, storemen, officers, masseurs, etc., etc., etc.

Because of my interest I was invited to join a Committee in Southampton formed in 1992 with the intention of bringing the liner back to the U.K. The "*Queen Mary* Project U.K." committee came into being when it was realised, after the Walt Disney Corporation suddenly pulled out from managing the ship (in all fairness theirs is a business of fantasy not of fact and historic preservation), that although general bids were being sought, the success of some bids would have meant a dreadful and disastrous end to an honourable vessel. Out of eighteen bids that from the U.K. Committee came within the last six to be considered when suddenly the ship was withdrawn from the market to be retained in Long Beach.

My interest is still keen with up to date information being received through friends and through the *Queen Mary* Foundation (who kindly invited me to become an honorary member) which maintains a close monitoring of changes made to the ship whilst encouraging her preservation.

It does still seem that "Concern" has to be the watchword at the present time, especially when economy - however important for her survival - overrules sympathetic use and even preservation.

To me - as she is to many hundreds and thousands of ex-passengers, crew, shipbuilders, troops who were transported in the ship, and to the many thousands more who admired and loved the liner from the shore - the *Queen Mary* is more than a magnificent ship, a superb enclave of art-deco artistry, a living example of the finest that British engineering and shipbuilding design and skill could achieve, a labour of love and sweat, of genius and supreme effort. She is a part of my past, of my upbringing and development, just as much as she is part of the present to those born in Long Beach since her arrival there over twenty five years ago.

She has given of her best and her best was legendary and because of that she surely deserves the best in return. She is unique. She is still, as King George V described her at her launch, ". . . . the stateliest ship now in being."

She is still our Queen.

Chapter 15

The Seduction of an Innocent
by Julian A. Hill

The writer of the Book of Proverbs lists four things that are too wonderful to be under-stood. One of these being 'the way of a man with a maid', and another 'the way of a ship in the midst of the sea'. I would combine these two in the form of a conundrum, namely, what is it that causes a highly intelligent and educated man to fall in love with a ship he has never seen and which is berthed in a far country thousands of miles away? For this is what happened to Julian Hill.
His introduction to the Queen Mary came through a book on the sinking of the Titanic. This led him to read a book about the Queen Mary, and there it was. Bingo! He was in love. Very soon he flew to Long Beach to see the object of his affection, and his feel-ings were confirmed and strengthened. He became involved in this country with a Consortium who put in a bid to bring her back to Britain, and he became a Director of The Queen Mary Foundation in Long Beach.
His infatuation with the Queen Mary may be difficult to understand, but like the man in Proverbs I find it wonderful. Read all about it!

My love of ocean liners began in 1989, when, as a gift, I was given Dr. Robert Ballard's book about his discovery of the wreck of the Titanic at the bottom of the Atlantic. Until I read this book, the scale and complexity of the engineering involved in the construction of ocean liners had com-pletely escaped me, and I had been equally ignorant of the opulence of their upper decks, so different from the hot, dirty, boiler rooms below.

Inspired by this discovery, I determined to find out more on the subject of liners. I was in a bookshop in Portsmouth one day when I saw another book about the Titanic on a shelf, together with a book about another liner called the *Queen Mary*. Having been brought up in London, and later living in Oxford, I had little experience of matters maritime, and the name "*Queen Mary*"

meant very little to me.

Contrary to expectation, it was the *Queen Mary* book (by David Hutchings) which turned out to be the more interesting of the two I bought that day. The *Queen Mary* was, much to my great astonishment, still appar-ently alive and well, moored in a place called Long Beach, on the other side of the world in California, and was being used as a hotel, conference centre and tourist attrac-tion. I had never expected that it would be possible actually to step on board a liner made before the war. Long Beach was a place I had to visit as soon as possible.

The reality was even better than the expec-tation. I first saw the *Queen Mary* at about 2 a.m. on a night in the summer of 1991. It is a moment I will never forget. I found the awe-some size of the vessel impossible to take in, but an attempt to walk the length of the ship taught me a lot about her.

I stayed in the hotel on the ship for a night or two, and it was as I gradually explored the numerous passageways and stairwells, as well as taking a guided tour through the engineering areas, swimming pool and what had been the catering areas, that I began to realise how much careful work and thought had gone into the construction of the *Queen Mary*. I had never before seen passageways, hundreds of feet long, lined with rich veneers. The beautifully decorated public rooms still displayed their specially commissioned artwork on the walls.

Many of the engineering spaces below the public area were cleared of machinery during the conversion work of the 1970s, when the *Queen Mary* was adapted for her new role as a permanently moored vessel. This was a great disappointment to me, as I had hoped to see something of the boiler rooms of such a powerful vessel. The aft engine room still remains however, and this area is largely as it was when the *Queen Mary* was in service. The huge turbines have not moved since that last day in 1967. The tree-like propeller shafts lie motionless now. What it used to be like to be in this vast area, so packed with hot, heavy machinery, when the ship was in motion (or even in a storm!) will always be left to my imagination.

I was so completely enthused by the sight of such a wonderful blend of engineering with British high class decor, that I bought a video camera and came back a week later to do it all again, but this time I caught it all on film to keep for posterity. Soon I was to go back to England, and I expected it would be a very long time indeed before I saw the *Queen Mary* again. How wrong I was.

Arriving back in England, I wondered at the time whether or not the citizens of Long Beach knew what a wonderful thing they had in the *Queen Mary*. I thought it rather sad if they did not, but never thought the ship could be under threat.

The Daily Telegraph of 4th November, 1991 carried an article about the *Queen Mary* Foundation, a non-profit organisation working in California to preserve the *Queen Mary* and to protect her from anyone who might wish to harm her. I decided that these were admirable aims, and joined this organisation as an overseas member.

It was not long after this that a friend came to my house with dire news: Had I heard that they were going to scrap the ship I had been to see? I thought he was joking, but the Daily Mail of 9th March, 1992 carried an article with the headline "That sinking feeling - Queen Mary faces the scrapyard". I made up my mind that this was not going to happen and telephoned the President of the *Queen Mary* Foundation that night to pledge my support.

It has always seemed incredible to me that Long Beach should even consider getting rid of such a landmark as the *Queen Mary*, but over the next twelve months, I saw quotations for scrapping and sinking the *Queen Mary* which demonstrated to me that the ship's future really was under consideration, and this was not a mere question of change of ownership.

At last, at the end of 1992, it was decided that the *Queen Mary* would stay in Long Beach and that ownership of the vessel would be transferred from The Port of Long Beach to The City of Long Beach. The new management is taking on an enormous task, and they do not have the resources of the Disney Company, who last acted as operators of the ship.

Now as a Director of the *Queen Mary* Foundation, I visit the ship at least once a year, and try to help her from this side of the Atlantic as much as I can. Eventually, it is my hope that British firms which helped in the construction of the *Queen Mary* between 1930-36, many of which are still in business, may one day be able to help a little with some aspects of her upkeep and restoration.

Whatever happens in the future, I would like to see the British connection with the *Queen Mary* maintained. Her Britishness is more than evident today, and I would encourage those who are interested in ships, or who have even travelled on the *Queen Mary* and have not seen her for some time, to visit her again.

Age cannot wither her, nor custom stale her infinite variety. She is still her stately self, and long may she remain so!

Chapter 16

The Queen Mary's Final Voyage
by John O. Smith

John Smith is the Senior Vice President of U.S. Merchant Marine Veterans World War II, an organisation founded in 1945 to bind together all those American merchant sailors who had braved and survived the might of Hitler's navy. They conceived the idea of acquiring a ship as a suitable memorial to their many comrades who had perished during the war, and the result was the "Lane Victory", which was handed over to the Veterans for restoration and refurbishment in 1989. Due largely to the enthusiasm, skill, and sheer hard work of John Smith and his colleagues, the "Lane Victory" is now restored and in sea-going condition, a remarkable achievement for senior citizens. The Veterans plan to sail her to Europe in June 1994 to take part in the 50 year celebration of D-Day.
In 1967 John Smith was appointed by the City of Long Beach as Survey Engineer for the Queen Mary, which they had recently acquired, and he came to Britain to familiarise himself with the ship. His account of the long voyage from Southampton to Long Beach makes fascinating reading.

It was a cold blustery morning on 31st October 1967, when the last passenger came aboard Cunard Line's Flagship, the R.M.S. *Queen Mary*, in Southampton, England, for the 40 day, 15,000 mile delivery trip to her new owners, the City of Long Beach, CA. With bands playing on ship and wharf, escorted by several Royal Naval ships and many vessels blaring their whistles, she sailed on a most eventful cruise at 11 a.m. on the short run to the first stop, Lisbon, Portugal. Despite the inclement weather, thousands of persons were on shore to bid farewell to a most historical liner that had been homeported there since her first voyage in 1936. She had made 1,001 North Atlantic crossings between Southampton and New York, carried about 3 million passengers, plus 800,000 America service people in World War II.

Loaded with a great quantity of supplies, 6,000 long tons of fuel oil, and 8,500 long tons of fresh water, she was using only two of her four 45,000 horsepowered engines to conserve fuel for the long passages between fuelling ports, and the schedule was set at 22 knots instead of her usual 28 plus knots. Too big to transit the Panama Canal or the Straits of Magellan, she was routed around Cape Horn with stops at Lisbon, Portugal; Las Palmas, Canary Islands; Rio de Janeiro, Brazil; Valparaiso, Chile; Callao, Peru; Balboa, Panama; and Acapulco, Mexico; with arrival at Long Beach, California scheduled for 9th December.

When the Cunard Line had decided to sell the ageing ship for scrap to the highest bidder in 1967, they were surprised and pleased to find that the successful bidder was the City of Long Beach, who planned to use her as a tourist attraction, and they were then very much surprised that the City proposed to carry passengers on the delivery voyage. Cunard officials had warned the buyers that much of the voyage would be in tropical waters and there was limited air conditioning aboard. A settlement was reached to carry only 1,200 passengers, about a third of her capacity. A travel agency was hired and quickly sold all the tickets to persons that were warned about the heat expected.

During the voyage the famous Cunard Line's reputation for excellent hospitality was evident, with gourmet food, great entertainment and service. The crew members were most co-operative and friendly, even though they would shortly be unemployed. Because of U.S. Immigration Laws, most of the crew would be returned to Southampton as soon as they arrived in Long Beach, and it would then be the City's responsibility to safeguard, operate, and maintain the 1,019 foot long vessel.

A phone call from the Long Beach Personnel Department, where I had previously sent in a résumé, resulted in a contract for me to go to Southampton sometime prior to the *Queen Mary*'s final departure as their Survey Engineer, and after arrival to be their Chief Operations Engineer. The first assignment was to learn the best location on the ship to hookup the various shoreside utility systems and the types and sizes of the connecting fittings that would be essential when the ship arrived in Long Beach, and to communicate this information as soon as possible to the city's engineering staff for the systems installation on the wharf before arrival, when the ship's 27 boilers would be shut down forever. Also included in the assignment was to learn about the ship's structure, security, stability, geographical layout, and the location, operation, and maintenance of the non-propulsive mechanical equipment and utility systems that would be needed after arrival.

After leaving Southampton the weather worsened, with big waves and strong winds and while crossing the Bay of Biscay, with all 4 stabilisers out, the ship was tossed about and very few persons showed up for meals. But all this was forgotten after arrival in the Tagus River, enroute to Lisbon, because of the big welcoming events that were going on with hundreds of welcoming vessels, including fireboats with water displays, and many cheering people lining the waterfront celebrating the first and last visit of the *Queen Mary*.

Portuguese dignitaries came aboard with invitations for events ashore, and had bottles of specially labelled commemorative Madeira Brandy for everyone aboard. Also a group of local entertainers came aboard to put on lengthy programmes in lounges.

This was typical of all the port visits, as a group of the City's public relations staff were to visit each stop in advance of the arrival, to gain publicity for the ship and her future home. They entertained the local press and electronic media with gifts, press kits, and tours of the ship and much food and beverages. Also on board was a full time P.R. man who sent out daily radio messages to the world's major news bureaux about the ship's progress, and even the most trivial event about the ship was broadcast so that by the time of arrival, the hype had created an almost hysterical atmosphere.

A regretful departure was made from Lisbon, and at sea on the short run to Las Palmas, Canary Islands, off the African coast, the weather and seas had moderated. In a smaller way, arrival at Las Palmas was enthusiastic and most people went on sightseeing trips around the beautiful island, or to the beaches. At the fuelling dock were several Spanish Naval Vessels, whose crew invited our crew members to visit their ships and had local wines and food in abundance. They also escorted the *'Mary'* to sea upon departure.

The 3,500 mile trip to Rio de Janeiro was in calm seas, but the heat began to increase daily, and most of us were sleeping topside in the comfortable deck chairs, and the two swimming pools were well occupied. Fortunately the 5 bars, 4 lounges and the dining rooms were air conditioned, so that no one had to miss any meals, entertainments or parties.

Crossing the equator was cause for a big celebration, with King Neptune initiating first timers into his kingdom, and then rewarding them with great quantities of champagne.

Arrival in Rio was a riotous event as the Governor had declared a holiday for the 'Queen's' arrival, and all kinds of vessels were circling about the beautiful bay, with noisy greetings, and it was quite difficult getting to the assigned anchorage. One tug boat blew her whistle so much that she lost steam to her engine, and had to be towed away. A mini Mardi-gras parade was put on for the passengers, and various other events were in progress ashore and on board. It was especially hot there and many persons got rooms at beach front hotels for the 3 day stay in Rio.

An almost continuous stream of small fuel oil, and water barges, as well as supply boats were coming alongside to replenish the ship for the next leg of the voyage. According to the officials, it was the largest quantity of ships supplies ever to be ordered there for one ship. A belated departure was made because ships officers had to clear the ship of stowaways.

During the voyage there were various entertainers coming and going at different stops, so that some new talent was always available. Besides local performers from the ports, there were several British musical comedy groups, as well as various Americans, including Johnny Mathis, Helen O'Connell, Robert Stack, Sarah Vaughn, and Bert Parks. The ship's orchestras were also playing in the various lounges, day and night.

After leaving Rio for the 3,900 mile voyage to Valparaiso, the temperature gradually lowered, and there were reports of a big storm at the southern tip of South America, but only moderate seas prevailed, with frequent rain squalls and fog. There was some concern aboard that because of poor visibility, the famous Cape Horn could not be seen. An earlier poll on the ship found that no one aboard had ever been there before, and some passengers stated that they only came on the voyage to see the Horn. Most fortunately the sun came out, and as if a curtain was lifted there was the spectacular sight on our starboard bow. A big cheer went up, whistles blew, bells rang, and cameras were clicking to preserve this once in a lifetime experience. Another celebration was put on by the cruise staff for this unique event, and a special Cape Horner's Certificate was given to all on board.

This was about the midway point of the voyage, and as the ship headed in a northerly direction for the first time on the trip, the seas built up and a regular gale was blowing, so the stabilisers went out again for the first time since Lisbon.

As we approached Valparaiso the seas moderated, but a potential problem was developing, as news arrived about a minor revolution going on at the nearby capital city of Santiago, and it might jeopardise the vessel's chance of getting the essential fuel, water, and other supplies, so that the voyage could continue.

Luckily the arrival was almost normal, except for a great deal of military activity going on ashore and in the harbor. The local people were exuberant in the welcoming ceremonies, and had several events going on for the visit, both ashore and aboard. However, there were warnings not to go on any tours out beyond the waterfront areas. Valparaiso was, and is, a Sister City of Long Beach, which had a lot to do with the co-operation of the officials and suppliers, as well as the good will of the general public.

After rounding up many would be stowaways, and sending them ashore, the ship left for Callao, Peru with moderate seas and temperatures prevailing. After a few pleasant days at sea Callao was reached, and the usual events were going on. Amongst the visitors coming aboard was the President of Peru, with many of his staff, and after the ceremonies were over he invited a large group of passengers and crew to visit him at his palace the next day in nearby Lima, the capital. However, the enormous native market was a better attraction. You could see skilled hand craftsmen making a great variety of interesting items, and you could bargain for almost anything from a solid gold toothpick in a leather case, to a 1,000 pound living Alpaca.

The usual round-up of would-be stowaways delayed the departure a bit, but the ship left before the tide dropped too much for the ship's draft to delay her sailing until the next high tide. At sea another big celebration was put on by the cruise director, and a special double shellback certificate was given to everyone for the second crossing of the equator.

During the voyage, at several stops, various Long Beach City Councilmen, the Mayor and Harbor Commissioners, would come aboard for certain segments of the trip, and all seemed pleased with their purchase. Also a few passengers had booked only certain parts of the voyage, and when they left, other people were ready to take their places.

Since leaving Callao the temperature had been climbing, and again the upper decks were occupied by sleepers at night. Alcoholic beverages were plentiful and cheap by American standards, and many parties were going on at all hours.

Each turn of the propellers moved the ship about 19 feet closer to her destination, and the 31 year old machinery and boilers were operating almost flawlessly. It was sad to think about their short future life. The two idle inside propellers had been disconnected from their engines before departure from England, and were rotating by the ship's movement, after a speed of about 5 knots was obtained. The engineering staff were justly proud of the vessel's performance during her final days.

Arrival at Acapulco was another major event, as a holiday had been declared for the ship's visit, and crowds were afloat and ashore with welcoming signs and greetings. A steady stream of passengers and crew were going ashore on the shore boats from the anchorage, and a steady stream of entertainers, dignitaries and ordinary people were coming on board to see the ship, as sort of an open house was declared for the last port visit. Also coming aboard were several City officials and key engineering assistants to learn their responsibilities after arrival in Long Beach. About 60 news reporters from the U.S. came aboard also, to publicise the final days of the liner's sea going career, and its new home. They were in a great celebrating mood with unlimited free beverages and no responsibilities until arrival.

Because of the open house policy in Acapulco there were a large number of stowaways aboard, and the ship's sailing was delayed until (hopefully) all of them were sent ashore.

The last leg of the voyage was an excuse for almost continuous celebrating, and the bartenders were most generous with the drinks. Many friendships had been formed during the voyage, and there were many regrets that the long cruise would soon be over. On the final night at sea, Captain J. Treasure Jones arranged for a giant nostalgic farewell party for everyone, with special cocktails, music, and entertainment, and short talks from ship's officers and passengers, and finally Captain Jones gave a very emotional farewell address, after which "Auld Lang Syne" was sung, and very few dry eyes were visible.

Shortly after daybreak we entered American waters, and a new Douglas DC-9 aeroplane flew over the ship, dipped its wings, and dropped thousands of beautiful flowers on deck as a welcoming gesture. As the liner continued up the California coast, the radar screen became almost completely blurred, as an enormous Armada of various types of vessels were approaching to welcome the *Queen Mary* to her new home, the City of Long Beach. The noise from the thousands of whistles, horns, bells and shouts was almost deafening, and on the shore line from Dana Point to Palos Verde Peninsular there was an estimated million persons to see the sight. Also overhead there were various military and civilian airlines, helicopters, and the Goodyear Blimp to add to the event.

The city's public relations people had done their job well, as there has probably never before been such an outpouring of nautical enthusiasm anywhere. After proceeding up to Point Fermin, the ship made a careful 'U' turn and went back to the Long Beach Harbor entrance to her temporary berth at Pier E, and after the engine room telegraph had wrung "Finished with Engines", the long historical voyage was over.

Enroute, the vessel had visited 4 Continents, and Ports in 8 Countries, passed through 8 time zones, rounded Cape Horn, crossed the equator twice, and arrived at her destination precisely on schedule, without any major problems with the ship, crew or passengers.

When the officials of Customs, Immigration, and Public Health were finished with their duties, disembarkation began with many tearful goodbyes from passengers and crew. At the same time new city employees were coming aboard to take over the big task of operating and safeguarding the giant prospect.

In a few days the last of her 27 boilers was shut down forever, and after a signing over meeting of Cunard and City Officials, the British flag was lowered and an American flag raised. When the R.M.S. *Queen Mary* was completely secured, the U.S. Coastguard declared the ship a floating building, and had no further jurisdiction over the "structure's" future.

At that moment the "building" entered into a completely new phase of its life, and it would always be a great challenge to equal the fantastic success of the previous 31 years.

Chapter 17

Looking Ahead to the Next Sixty Years
by David Rubin

David Rubin is a founder member and an ex-President of the Queen Mary Foundation. He is noted for three things - his utter devotion to the ship, his energy, and his forthright behaviour. To David a spade is a spade - or rather an anchor is an anchor - and he has demonstrated a tremendous capacity for hard work and determination on behalf of the Queen Mary. We all owe much to him. I am pleased to provide this opportunity for David to express his opinions, but must make it clear that his views, and indeed the views of all my other contributors, are not necessarily shared by us all!

The *Queen Mary* today is a precious link with the past, for this magnificent ship has survived whereas many of her predecessors have long since gone. She is the last remaining survivor of an age when travel by ocean was a glamorous affair, when money was no object and when going from America to Great Britain or Great Britain to America was a leisurely adventure, not a fast paced jaunt.

Today the *Queen Mary* is recognised throughout the world, not only because she is the last of the great North Atlantic liners from the 1930's, but because she holds such wondrous treasures of art, decoration, and design. And while the economic times of the day dictate that she must be able to carry her own weight, she does not because the beauty which made her world renowned from the 1930's until the 1960's is not displayed or even properly maintained.

On this the sixtieth year of the anniversary of her launch, the *Queen Mary* deserves more than what she has been given. What the *Queen Mary* deserves from us is our respect. She also deserves to be seen once again with pride and the dignity befitting a liner of her status. However, in deserving all

of these things, she also needs to survive for sixty more years but not in her present condition and not being handled as she is now.

What is needed for this last ocean greyhound is preservation, restoration, and a continuous period of ongoing twenty-four hour maintenance as might be necessary. To this end new and radical thinking must be employed in her future. What the *Queen Mary* needs now is vision and not just simple vision, but the vision that says that what worked before to make her great can work again.

Therefore, the future of the *Queen Mary* should be that of preservation and restoration. These factors once implemented will make people desire to see her again and to experience what it was like to live for five days on one of the greatest ocean liners of the twentieth century. And while she may never sail again, this does not mean that those amenities that made her service famous cannot be put into her once again.

Once these have been accomplished, then a program of continuous maintenance must be implemented and rigorously maintained. Much has been neglected in twenty-six years and she is in need of a great deal of love and care. Also those ideas that required her structural alteration only to fail, need to be rectified so that she may continue to physically survive for another sixty years.

Once these three factors have been achieved, and only by employing these three factors will the *Queen Mary* once again have pride and proper respect she deserves. However, there are those who may ask, can these factors be accomplished? And the answer is that they can but to do so will require support that has never been given before, new methods that have never been tried before, and a tough, dedicated group to accomplish what should have been an ongoing process.

Much will need to be done to erase twenty-six years of mistakes, failures and misguided programs. The *Queen Mary* will need to be pampered during these stages and there will be no room for further mistakes. This task will not be for the faint of heart or for those who may never see the light at the end of the tunnel. The light is there, but to reach it much murkiness must first be crossed before even the first glimmer is seen.

Whereas the planners and builders of the *Queen Mary* gave way to the officers and crews who guided her through thirty-one years of service, these men and women in turn gave way to new owners, operators, "crews", enthusiasts, and onlookers. But for any real hope for the return of the *Queen Mary*, this second group must give way to the movers and shakers, the doers - the preservationists who will take the *Queen Mary* and give her what she needs to compete financially in the twenty-first century, a combination of Respect, Dignity, and a Pride through Preservation, Restoration, and Maintenance.

In restoring the *Queen Mary* not only will the last great transatlantic liner of the 1930's be restored but a part of the history of the North Atlantic will be restored and brought to the forefront of maritime preservation. In restoring this mighty vessel it will be a tribute to the men and women who designed, built, worked, travelled, and served in her. In restoring the *Queen Mary* a time of peace will be reflected when things were simpler and the art of travel had reached its highest peak in speed, luxury, and performance. And in restoring the *Queen Mary* a sense of pride and achievement will once again be displayed in helping to return to the present the grandeur and beauty of the past.

Chapter 18

The preservation of a Legend
by Robin B. Jacobs

Robin Jacobs is an extraordinary man. He is by profession a Model Maker and Precision Engineer, and his standards are those of a perfectionist. Robin's working models of the Queen Mary's propulsion and other equipment have to be seen to be believed.

His skills in working in both metal and wood extend to the building of much larger objects than models, and are backed by a profound and detailed knowledge of the ship as she was in 1936. He must inevitably have an important part to play in any plans for her restoration and preservation.

For the record, he now owns his own business, designing and fabricating working models, wood furniture, and various metal projects.

My interest in ships began when I was a small boy. I've always been fascinated as to how ships floated and moved through the water and wondered what propelled them. I can remember building toy boats from odds and ends around the house, each one being larger than the one before it. It wasn't until May, 1971, when the *Queen Mary* was opened to the public, that my love for ships really grew. I will never forget the impact that first visit to the great ship made upon me! I was amazed by her size and splendour!! I have been aboard dozens of ships since then, but no other has ever captured my attention and generated as much of my enthusiasm as the *Queen Mary* has done. That day, back in 1971, changed my life for, as I left the *Queen Mary*, I felt as if I had found my "calling" and that I was destined to somehow be involved in her future.

I soon began reading (and collecting) books, and artifacts pertaining to her. This has now grown into a small library, which contains over 300 blueprints, as well. My fascination for mechanical science has fueled my intense research of the *Queen Mary* for more than 20 years. This same research has taken me beyond just the areas of the passenger accommodations, and has allowed me to see, and gain knowledge of, a side of the ship few people ever study. I have discovered several "bits and pieces" of information (some rare, some rather bizarre), but most being useful for a project I was planning in the future.

One of my long-term engineering goals has been to design and build an exact 1/4 scale, working model of the *Queen Mary*. This model has become my best technological achievment, and has been a labor-of-love for the ship and the working trades. It was designed to be a complete working model, capable of sailing under her own power, with over 300 functions. I began laying the keel in 1983, using original (as built) shipyard drawings, depicting the way she appeared in 1936. This model is 22 feet long and will weigh nearly 2000 pounds when completed.

She features 3 water tube boilers which will supple steam to 4 sets of turbines, each independently driving its own propeller.

Over the last twenty years, I have visited the ship hundreds of times and have probably gone to just about every area one can go. Each time, I feel the overwhelming potential the ship really has! Even in the gutted machinery spaces, I see great possibilities! These spaces as they are today, are "eerie" and mysterious to visit and truly offer a one-of-a-kind exploring experience. However, they could offer so much more to the visitor if properly developed. There seems to always be a large number of people who are interested in touring these spaces. In my experience of giving tours, the young and old alike are truly awe-stricken, full of quesions and hungry for information. I have never met anyone who hasn't been impressed after seeing the sheer size of the boiler rooms, and the machinery spaces! The boilers, alone, were the single most vital pieces of machinery on board and truly the heart of the ship. Few people realise that steam was not only provided for propelling the ship, but was also used for other services. Without steam, there would be no electricity for pumps, ventilation, heating, refrigeration, cooling, drinking water, or cooking! Although the *Queen Mary* is no longer in service, I feel the importance of her boilers should be recognised.

For several years, different plans and ideas have come up for developing the *Queen Mary*'s remaining boiler rooms into usable space. It is my strong opinion that this would be the single greatest mistake tha owners and operators of the ship could make.! Since the city gutted her machinery spaces in 1969, the attitude has been that they are nothing but large, empty rooms waiting to be filled. I think one needs to take a serious look at the historic value these spaces possess. They represent the very heart and soul of the ship!! These spaces are extremely important to the ship's past and, I think, should in no way be developed into anything other than the purpose for which they were intended. The *Queen Mary* has the distinction of having the largest machinery spaces ever to be put aboard any ship and her boilers would require a space nearly a football field in length! Visitors need to be able to experience the feeling of walking through these cavernous rooms and explore

the unique setting, which cannot be found anywhere else but on the *Queen Mary*!

There is growing interest in a plan that I have for restoring one, or more, of the ship's four remaining boiler rooms, along with one of her turbo generator rooms. The plan would be to build six full scale reproductions of her water-tube boilers and install them in one of the remaining boiler rooms. I have tested the feasibility of this plan by building an exact scale, working model of one of the ship's water tube boilers. From this, I have come to the conclusion that it would, in fact, be feasible to build full size replicas exactly as they originally appeared in 1936! These boiler reproductions could most likely be built in modular sections, of wood and covered in special insulation panels to simulate the boiler's casing. Discarded valves, gauges etc. could be purchased from local scrapyards. Other auxilary machinery and fittings could be reproduced, in a historically accurate manner. Along with proper lighting and sound effects, the "mock" boilers could be brought to life to give the visitor an impressive visual and audio experience. This would give the public a very realistic demonstration as to what it must have been like to have been in the boiler rooms at full steam! The bridge walkway running between boiler rooms number 3 and 4, would provide an excellent passage leading through the boiler's up-takes, passing up from the boilers to the funnel hatch. This would also provide a rare opportunity to view the interior of the boiler up-takes, as well as the tops of boiler 5, themselves. Vantage points could be gained from different areas off the working alleyways. White suited boiler firemen might be used to give demonstrations, showing the way in which the boilers were fired. They might lead tours through the boiler room and machinery spaces, giving detailed facts and figures about the areas being viewed. The history of the steam boilers could be explained, stating how they were developed over the years, along with stories about the stokers and the dreadful conditions under which they worked.

Only one of the ship's two turbo-generator rooms is still intact. Unfortunately, the generators and auxiliary machinery have long since been removed. The importance of electricity, and the way in which it was generated, needs to be emphasized. In my opinion, it would be quite feasible to build full-sized wooden replicas of her generators and restore her forward turbo-generator room exactly as it appeared originally. This would give visitors a lasting impression as to how the "once-world's-largest, floating power station" appeared. Here again, proper lighting and sound effects of the generators and machinery running would make a dramatic impact on tourists!

My main objective with this plan is to bring to attention exactly how the boiler rooms and machinery spaces could be used, in a historically correct manner. This would also generate revenue and become a major attraction! Most of us have one thing in common... we enjoy exploring and being intrigued. This would be a great opportunity upon which the operators of the ship could capitalize! The boiler model (which I constructed) and is currently on display in the *Queen Mary*'s Museum, gives a three-dimentional, futuristic display of the way in which these rooms could be developed.

My philosophy regarding the *Queen Mary* is really quite simple... give the public what they want, they will feel satisfied, and they will return again and again! The people who visit the ship expect to experience her luxury and explore her history. They also expect to see and feel a 1930's Ocean Liner atmosphere. But when they come aboard and see areas that are neglected and run-down, the feeling is usually one of disappointment. In the past 20 years that I have been associated with the ship, many people have told me of their disappointment and wonder why many areas are in poor condition, and why something isn't done to remedy the situation. If people visiting the ship feel that way about her appearance, we can pretty much expect they won't be coming back for another visit! Negative public reactions have a way of spreading around and can be very damaging. Overcoming the public's impression about the ship's condition can, of course, be changed, and the number of people returning to re-visit the ship can be increased quite considerably!

Since her retirement from service, the public has seen only the shell of the great ship she once was. It is essential to the ship's survival and lasting success that a restoration program be started soon. Restoring parts of the ship to it's original condition would allow visitors to experience her opulence,

atmosphere and lifestyle, which are now of a buygone era. One of the major complaints that I have most often heard, is that there is not enough activities and amenities for the hotel guests. They often leave the ship in the evening in search of entertainment in town. That money could have been spent aboard the ship but is spent elsewhere! Therefore, hotel amenities need to be added, to encourage the guests to remain on board for activities and amusement.

A swimming pool is one basic amenity that can be found in most hotels and motels on land. The *Queen Mary* has one of the most lavish swimming pools ever built within a ship and when in service, it was extremely popular with the passengers. Restoring the ship's pool area and bringing it up to state regulations for hotel guests to use, would be a very important attraction.

Other amentities for hotel guests could include a gymnasium and Squash Racketball Court, both constructed in their original locations on the Sundeck. Deck tennis courts and shuffleboard (historical shipboard games) could be offered for recreation.

Tea-Time was always a popular pastime and could be re-introduced to guests staying aboard. Tea and drinks could be served by Stewards to hotel guests lounging in reproduction deck chairs, arranged in rows on the Prom Deck. One of my recent projects for the ship has been the construction of a prototype of one of the *Queen Mary*'s original deck chairs. The ship is now featuring it as a sales model display for taking orders from customers in the ship's Drawing Room. My hope with this project is that someday the ship will want additional reproductions of this deck chair in which the hotel guests could lounge. Having deck chairs available for guests on an hourly rental basis, could generate revenue for the ship. This would also help boost Bar and pastry sales, while bringing back one of the oldest of all shipboard traditions.

Primarily, the restoration should first be carried out in the locations which directly come into contact with the public. However, there are a number of locations on the lower decks which should be considered. I am in agreement with Ron Winter that the Working Alleyway on 'C' Deck needs to be restored! This Working Alleyway was the main artery of the ship's anatomy – a "lifeline" which connected the ship's crew with all of the working spaces on the ship. Also known as the "Burma Road", this main companionway ran fore and aft on the port side of 'D' Deck (now 'C' Deck), for a length of 614 feet. Hidden from passengers on the lower decks, it served as a vital link, enabling the crew to get to the different locations. Thus, they could carry out their work without infiltrating the passenger spaces.

Off this alleyway, there was access to all of the main storerooms; pantries; cold storage area; meat and poultry store; Plumber's shop; Carpenter's shop; Machine shop; Electrician's shop; Print shop; Hospital; Dental Office; Crew's Gallery; Engineer's Dining Room; Steward's Accommodations; Crew's Cabins; and Leading Greaser's Mess.

I'm very optimistic concerning the *Queen Mary*'s future! I refuse to believe she cannot become a successful, profitable attraction! If those of us who care about her well-being can continue to work together, these restoration projects will become a money-making reality! I feel most fortunate to have been able to contribute (in a small way) towards this endeavor. I sincerely hope my ideas and thoughts will help to inspire others, with ideas, to become involved

It is of vital importance that we realise the *Queen Mary* is the last of her kind! Built at the height of the Trans-Atlantic Liner period, she marked the beginning of a new era of passenger comfort and style. The ending of her career on the Atlantic was the most symbolic of them all, for this was also the end of a long and cherished era, the likes of which the world will never see again! She was built during the years when people took pride in the quality of their work, and craftsmanship really mattered! There was a special bond between the *Queen Mary* and those who helped build her. The workers poured their hearts and souls into the construction of this great ship. To this day, no ship has ever been built with such a "Labor of Love"!

The *Queen Mary* is a very complex, technological masterpiece – a monument to man's ingenuity and creativity. Unequaled, she is, without doubt, the greatest maritime achievement of all time! And although the craftsmen of those days may be gone, their gifts to all of us live on in the great architectural achievements of the world. It is important that the *Queen Mary* endure for the benefit of future generations to enjoy. She offers something for everyone... history, nostalgia, beauty, power, strength and mystery. Her designers and builders left a rare treasure for us to respect and appreciate. Her legacy to us must and will continue to live on if her future stays in the hands of those who care, and recognise what a splendid gift her craftsmen left for the world to admire.

Chapter 19

My Contact with History
by Maria DuBry

As a schoolgirl Maria DuBry remembers the excitement of the Queen Mary's arrival in Long Beach. Little did she think that when she grew up she would work aboard the ship, but for the last four years now the Queen Mary has been her *ship, and she has revelled in it. For Maria's job as Administrative Assistant in the Office of Pacifica Speciality Tours aboard the Queen Mary requires her to know the ship and be able to share her knowledge and enthusiasm with visitors. The ship could not have a better advocate, as those of us who were lucky enough to attend the 59th Anniversary of the launch soon found out. Maria probably spends as much time aboard the Queen Mary as anyone else, so that her opinion is particularly important and interesting.*

What is it like to report to work every day on one of the greatest ocean liners ever built? Even though She is permanently docked, the *Queen Mary* remains a magnificent sight as I pull into the adjacent parking lot. Because I open our offices at seven a.m. I often glimpse many spectacular views not seen by the later arriving tourists. I have seen our Grand Lady shrouded in fog so thick the only visible parts are the tip tops of the massive smokestacks peeking through. Or with golden pink highlights reflecting off the stern as the sunrise is mirrored in the many portholes.

As I walk the gangway to board, I never fail to think, however fleeting, of the many people who have walked this path before me. I am placing my feet in the very same spots as film stars and royalty. Even the most routine office errand can become an adventure if you pass through the magnificence of the art-deco first class pool area as you deliver a mundane memo to the sales department. The corridors can seem endless, and I am still, after a year, finding new nooks and crannies

to explore. Elevators creak and groan as they take you through stark crew only access ways, so different from the opulent public areas of the ship. When it's break time, how many workers can perch on the Foredeck anchor chains and watch seagulls against a fluffy cloud filled sky?

As an employee I have access to areas that are off limits to regular visitors. The dim cavernous holds that once contained massive boilers and engines can be very eerie even during the day. One of my most special memories of this area occurred during a tour given to one of the ships designers, Dr. John Brown. Because of his age (92) it was felt Dr. Brown would not want or be able to walk the narrow dimly lit plankways that connect the boiler rooms to the forward cargo holds. When it was suggested that we not go further forward, he surprised us all by eagerly voicing a request to continue onward. He completed this journey in slow but grand style carefully inspecting "his" holds and their current state. While he reminisced about the building and testing of the ship,

Dr. Brown's voice echoed off the five story walls forming an unforgettable memory for me. After the tour we all adjourned to the bar for Margaritas!

Working on the *Queen Mary* is much more than a job. It's a daily experience in history and artistic craftsmanship that will never be matched. And they pay me for it too! How dull it will be if I ever have to go back to working in an office bounded by four walls, instead of an environment limited only by my imagination!

Chapter 20

Long Live the Queen
by Leo Greene

Leo Green has a different background to any of my other contributors, for he was for some time Administrative Assistant to the City Manager of Long Beach. He therefore saw the Queen Mary from a very privileged point of view, that of a representative of the owners, and in this position he was able to make a unique assessment of the value of the ship to the City, the Community, and indeed the World.
He too was present on the long last cruise from England to Long Beach, and became convinced that she must be preserved. He became President of the old Queen Mary Club, and has made around 400 speeches in support of the ship. It is not surprising therefore that the following article condemns timid critics and advocates bold and imaginative policies.

In marking the Tenth Anniversary of the arrival of the *Queen Mary* in Long Beach, we saluted an event that for good or for bad, made the name of the City of Long Beach known in every civilised country on the globe. A dozen years before, the average citizen of our city had to explain its existence as being a seaport just twenty miles south of Los Angeles. Today, the *Queen Mary* has made the name of Long Beach as distinguished and individual as New York, New Orleans, Marseilles or Athens. World-wide, Long Beach is known as the home of the *Queen Mary*.

The *Queen Mary* has achieved many records: she held the record for fast crossings of the Atlantic for years; she was fondly remembered as an incomparable troop carrier during the years of WWII, publicly praised by Churchill for having shortened the war by as much as a year through her ability to move armies around the world. She was synonymous with the ultimate in luxury, class and service as a trans-Atlantic liner,

and the symbol of recovery to a depression-ridden Britain in the '30's. Most of all, she remains the epitome of imagination and daring through her conversion as a maritime museum, Hotel, restaurant, bar, tourist and convention center.

From her very beginning, the *Queen Mary* has been the target of little minds and timid souls. She was too big, too expensive, too different to ever be worth her cost. She proved her critics wrong by being the most successful liner in the Atlantic. When War came, her use as a transport was condemned: her loss would mean the loss of an entire regiment plus the ship. Yet she survived gloriously, despite the promise of a fortune to any U-boat commander who would sink her,. She sailed into the very teeth of danger, and escaped unscathed because she was the *Queen Mary*! Finally, she was sold to Long Beach as a means of promoting Long Beach. Today, her name and the city's name are synonyms for each other. The cost of her conversion, excessive though it might have been, has been exceeded many fold by the publicity she has generated.

That cost has been made the basis of political campaigns, special interest drives, and a target of public dissatisfaction with individuals and policies. It has been attacked as a boondoggle, as a waste of public funds, as a deliberate fraud upon the people. Yet, it is seldom pointed out that the ship has not cost a penny of tax money. Its purchase and conversion were paid for by Tideland revenues, every cent of which was audited and re-audited by departmental, City and State auditors. Every cent expended was approved as lawful and proper by the State Lands Commission. Every cent was certified as being in the interest not just of Long Beach but of every citizen in the State of California.

The Tideland revenues are declining. Yet does anyone suppose that if the money expended upon the *Queen Mary* were held by the City in a special fund, that that fund would have been safe from a sudden raid by the State legislature to underwrite some other program? How many recall the Mallon decision, and the more than $120 millions it cost the City of Long Beach? Why are not some of these critics asking for that decision to be reviewed by the United States Supreme Court, when our own State Supreme Court was split 4 to 3 on the final decision? But, no! It is far too easy to make the *Queen Mary* the target of their wrath and criticism. They forget how many times the ship has made fools of her critics before this.

The *Queen Mary* has been the victim of her exploiters. The City has forgotten the original purpose for her purchase. The book-keepers and the auditors have taken over, looking only at the bottom line, seeking the last possible cent of profit out of every transaction regardless of whether or not a profit might be realised in more than a fiscal manner. It complicated the situation by splitting control of the ship between four non co-operative entities. While owned by the City, the municipality has little or no control over the activities of other lessors. So long as the control is divided, so long as the operation is marked by non co-operation, so long as the owner allows the renters to control policies, the ship will be in trouble and a constant source of criticism. Only when she is removed from politics, from the continuous campaigning slogans of councilmanic members and candidates, when the City Manager no longer has to justify his actions with regard to the ship, when a single body, autonomous and independent is given control of all aspects of the vessel, can the *Queen Mary* come into her own.

The ship has a potential life of 300 years. With the passage of very year she becomes more valuable and unique. She is a frozen moment of the luxurious life of the 1930's; she is a living part of the crisis filled days of WWII; she is a symphony of the marine architect, the artist, the sculptor, and the deco moderne art of the first half of the twentieth century. She is a moment of history caught as is an insect in amber, perfect and beautiful and complete. We owe it to future generations, those future descendants whom we have deprived of their share of fossil fuels and wealth, the treasure for which we traded their birthright. Leaders may rise and fall, generations may come and go, critics may rage and rail, but none has the right to deprive the future of the treasure we possess: none has the right to decide that what has been expended shall be thrown to the winds, that the *Queen Mary* shall be destroyed because she is not a profit item.

As well destroy the Eiffel Tower, the Statue of Liberty, the Pyramids and the Sphinx. What is their basic value as scrap? What is their spiritual value? Just so, we must give attention to the true values of the *Queen Mary*, what she means not only today but tomorrow and tomorrow's tomorrow. The Colossus of Rhodes, one of the wonders of the ancient world, finally ended as scrap carried away on the backs of 900 camels. The world was the loser. Let such a tragedy never be repeated with the *Queen Mary*!

Chapter 21

Clydebank, Birthplace of Queens
by Provost Alastair Macdonald J.P.

In 1993 Alastair Macdonald was Provost (or Mayor) of Clydebank in Scotland, and as such was their No. 1 'Bankie', and ambassador. At the 59th Anniversary Celebrations he impressed everyone with his sincerity and enthusiasm for a continuing and growing contact between his fabulous town and the City of long Beach, a contact that springs from, and is cemented by, the presence of the Queen Mary at the centre of the Long Beach tourist industry.
Clydebank will always be remembered as the birthplace of the Queens and many other splendid ships, and their inhabitants have won world wide renown for their work. Personally, I regard it as a great honour once to have been described by the Provost as "one who should have been a 'Bankie'".
I precede the following article by Alastair about Clydebank by quoting an extract from the speech he made on board the Queen Mary on Sunday 26 September 1993, a speech that was extremely well received by all who heard it.

"Mayor Kell, Mr. Prevratil, Honoured Guests, Ladies and Gentlemen. As Provost of Clydebank, may I say that I am absolutely delighted to be with you here today. This is a thrill and a pleasure I had not dreamed of experiencing barely three weeks ago.

I would like to place on record my appreciation for this invitation to three people in particular - to Diane Rush, Lisa Lynn Backus, and of course the boss himself, Joseph F. Prevratil. To all three of you a big thank you for making this day possible. I would also wish to place on record my heartfelt thanks to the many others I have been privileged to meet who have made this day such a memorable occasion.

Ladies and Gentlemen, the Clydebank of today is a far cry from the Clydebank which gave birth to so many magnificent ships and the greatest of them all, this lady which we honour this morning. But although our engineering skills have been channelled in other directions - although our shipbuilding skills are used constructing oil platforms - although much has changed - Clydebank is and always will be in the hearts of Scots men and women throughout the world, the town of the Three Queens - *The Queen Elizabeth, The QE2* and the Queen of them all - The *Queen Mary*.

And so it is with the good wishes of all my fellow citizens in Clydebank, and the good wishes of Scottish shipbuilders and "Bankies" throughout the world, that I stand before you today. We are proud of our achievements - we are very happy that The *Queen Mary* has found a good and permanent home amongst the people of Long Beach - amongst the people who share our pride in the greatest ship ever built.

I am privileged to be an Honorary Member of the Retired Boilermakers Union on The

Clydeside and many of them worked on the *Queen Mary*. When they heard I was coming out here, some of them told me to say 'hello' to the Lady they still love. I shall be able to tell them I have carried out their request, and that she is happy and in good condition amongst friends.

It is also with open arms that we welcome the proposals to participate in a sister city relationship between Long Beach and Clydebank. I carry with me today the fraternal greetings of my Council and the people of Clydebank who wish you every success in this venture and whatever the future has to offer.

Ladies and Gentlemen, you have a city to be proud of and you honour us by participating in this affair. I have only been with you three days but from now on I will consider myself an adopted brother of Long Beach. Had my fellow Councillors been privileged to what I have enjoyed over the past few days they would have been asking me why we didn't adopt Long Beach as a Sister City long ago."

The above remarks made in September 1993 during a nostalgic visit to the R.M.S. *Queen Mary* in Long Beach, California, contrast modern Clydebank, centrally situated in the West of Scotland with excellent communication links to the rest of the United Kingdom and Europe by road, rail and sea, and less than fifteen minutes from Glasgow's International Airport, with the older shipbuilding community which grew up on green fields along the bank of the River Clyde - perhaps the most famous shipbuilding river in the world. Nowadays, Clydebank has very close and rapidly developing trading facilities with the European Community and indeed, throughout the world, with a reputation for international experience and marketing expertise which, I believe, is second to none in Scotland.

This heritage, of which we are justly proud, did not arise overnight, nor for that matter by accident, but began in 1871 when the shipbuilders, James and George Thomson moved their Yard down river from an overcrowded Glasgow environ to the green fields of "Barns O'Clyde" on the ground opposite the mouth of the River Cart. Such was the beginning of "Tamson's Toon". In later years Thomson's "Clydebank" yard became better known as John Brown's after its take-over by the Sheffield steelmakers of

that name - a name which will be forever stamped indelibly over the history of shipbuilding throughout the world.

Brown's Clydebank Yard gave birth to some of the largest, finest and fastest ships ever built - the greatest of which, undoubtedly, were our "three Queens". The elegant *Queen Mary* launched in 1934, her sister ship *Queen Elizabeth* launched in 1938, and the *QE2* launched in 1967, were the culmination of developments in shipbuilding design and were preceded by the beautiful Cunarders *Lusitania* and *Aquitania*. The *Queen Mary* - now an American "national monument" - and the *QE2* remain today a magnificent embodiment of the technological expertise for which Clydebank has become deservedly famous. The coming of shipbuilding to Clydebank, therefore, not only gave rise to Clydebank as a town but also saw the origins of a workforce famed for craftsmanship, engineering skills and a long tradition of maritime technology.

Sadly, to-day the once proud legend of "Clydebuilt" has passed into history and our unsurpassed reputation for heavy engineering and shipbuilding has been sacrificed at the alter of financial greed, political apathy and industrial arrogance. Whilst ships are no longer built in Clydebank the engineering traditions are still maintained by John Brown Engineering and U.I.E. who jointly occupy the yard and have adapted for the construction of sophisticated gas turbines and oil and gas rigs respectively servicing countries throughout the globe.

The Clydebank of the 1990's is a far cry from the town where the clang of metal upon metal, the chatter of the riveters hammer and the spark of welders torches were constant reminders of our lifeblood and yet, even now, the intense feelings which shipbuilding engenders in Clydebank hostelries borders almost on the religious experience. I have often been in the company of some of those old welders, riveters and caulkers when their eyes would glaze over (not from the drink) but in memory of their shipbuilding days.

Without a shadow of a doubt, the favourite of them all was the *Queen Mary*. The stories which surround her on-off construction are a legend on Clydeside and everyone of that generation would claim to have played a part in her construction. Perhaps more than any other vessel, the people of Clydebank took the *"Mary"* to their hearts. It is true to say that during a period of national economic hardship the work created by the Mary literally fed and clothed thousands of families on the Clyde. Is it any wonder she was much revered?

In 1980 when I was first elected as a member of Clydebank District Council, I was given a special recognition, the title, "Honorary Member of the Retired Boilermakers Association for the Clyde". To this day I am proud of this title.

In 1993 I was invited as Provost of Clydebank District to attend the 59th anniversary of the *Queen Mary*, part of a week of civic celebrations. This event coincided with efforts to establish a "sister city" relationship between the communities of Clydebank and Long Beach. The excitement expressed and encouragement given by, the entire Clydebank community and the shipbuilding fraternity, in particular, was overwhelming. If best wishes for my journey could have been transferred into pound notes, I would have been a very wealthy man indeed.

On Sunday, 26 September, at precisely 11.00 am. I marched with chest out, head held high and a swagger to my step in company with the distinguished designer of the *Queen Mary*, Dr. John Brown; the senior electrical officer, Ron Winter and a former shipwright, George Kean, to the tune of "Scotland the Brave" behind a pipe band along the decks of the old lady. For that brief moment I was the proudest man on earth and wouldn't have changed positions with anyone.

In the early hours of that never to be forgotten day, restless and excited at the prospect of making my first public speech in America, I wandered along the deserted foot-worn teak decks, touching and caressing metal and wood which the skills of Clydebank men and women had transformed into a work of industrial art. I could almost imagine this creation to have a life and that a heart still beat softly within its shell. My thoughts, inevitably, turned to some of my boilermaker friends - my heart almost burst with pride and tears began to run, unashamedly, down my cheeks as I visualised the faces of my pals whose contributions assisted in the creation of this wonderful lady.

I shall always be grateful for the opportunity and privilege of visiting and living on board the *Queen Mary* in her new home in Long Beach. I shall never be able to adequately voice my feelings towards the greatest ship ever built but after that visit I do now understand why these old shipyard pals of mine talked in terms of reverence, with emotion and occasionally, with a watery look in their eyes. I now know why I cried. I now know why the name of Clydebank and the *Queen Mary* will forever remain symbols of excellence and enterprise wherever ships sail or shipyard workers gather.

In her comfortable home beneath the warm Californian sun, on behalf of the people of Clydebank I wish the *Queen Mary* a "long and happy retirement".

Chapter 22

The Positive Image of Long Beach
by Lisa Lynn Backus

The whole responsibility for organising the 59th anniversary celebration was borne by Lisa Lynn Backus, and she delighted us all by the efficiency and smooth running of the event. We were also amazed at her stamina, for after travelling to Europe to collect us all and escort us to Long Beach, she then worked tirelessly during the visit to ensure our comfort.

Lisa Lynn runs her own business - Pacifica Speciality Tours - aboard the Queen Mary, and organises many Conventions and Special Events such as ours. Her love affair with the Queen Mary began several years ago, and she was one of the principal fighters in 1992 when there seemed to be no future in Long Beach for the ship. Thank goodness there are people like Lisa Lynn Backus about when adversity threatens.

The following account is extracted from a letter she wrote to me recently.

When I first became involved in the 'fight' for 'saving' the *Queen Mary*, it was because (1) the majority of my business came from visitors to the ship, (2) I didn't want the City to lose out on many wonderful memories and revenue brought to Long Beach, and (3) I watched on Cable TV as a few *Queen Mary* employees testified and begged for help to the City Council. I also read letters to the editor of the Press-Telegram, our local daily newspaper, from a lady named Michelle White, who was one of those employees. I decided to write my own letter, and soon after met about 10 people who became a core group with this cause as our unifying goal. We gave up much of our personal lives to testify before the Harbor Commission every Monday afternoon and at lengthy (sometimes 12 hours!) City Council meetings every Tuesday, We researched tirelessly, reading report after report. We were continually criticised, berated, condemned and verbally abused by those on the 'other

side', and by many who were just of an opposing opinion. The worst part was that most of these detractors just lacked the right information to make sound judgements.

Anyway, it was this process that began my love for the ship.

I truly believe that just about everyone and certainly anyone has a personal relationship with the *Queen Mary*.

I continually meet people who helped in her construction, who worked on her as a cruise ship, who sailed on her in the war, who were sailing on another ship as the Mary passed them by at great speed, who were war brides who travelled to their new U.S home aboard her, and more. And, of course, there were those of us who have made the ultimate commitment to see her through these last few years, what perhaps may have been her toughest battle yet.

It was while meeting these people that I approached Mr. Prevratil on the ideas that I wanted to implement for the 59th

Anniversary of the Launch event. Mr. Prevratil, understanding my level of desire and commitment, agreed and "gave me the green light."

I made my first official trip to Scotland in June of 1993, compliments of American Airlines, and I met up with George Kean who graciously toured me around the John Brown Shipyard where the ship was built. I found George probably the funniest man I'd ever met, and his wife Betty and their daughter and her family were just delightful.

Following my return to the U.S., I continued to correspond with George and others in Clydebank. Most of the credit for the support I received on that end go to John Hood, Chief Librarian of the Clydebank District. Without his on-the-record and off-the-record help, and his convincing the Provost to accept my September invitation to Long Beach, the 59th Anniversary event would not have been.

Through this all, among my strongest corporate allies were American Airlines and Cunard. They are to be commended for believing in me, the *Queen Mary*, and the value of international coalition building. American sent me twice to the U.K. for special promotion, international goodwill, and to spread the good word that the *Queen Mary* was still in Long Beach and still open for the public to enjoy. And, of course, the secondary message was that American can fly you right into Long Beach from the U.K., with only one simple plane change. Diane Rush, President of the *Queen Mary* Foundation, was my link to the guts of the ship and to its builders. It was through her that I first learned of the nine people I would soon come to be escorting from the U.K. to Long Beach for the September ceremonies.

It was her research the year before (and Hal Johnson's in 1979), that was the catalyst for the event I had planned. I just needed to find a funding source.

Once again I turned to American Airlines who agreed to donate round trip tickets from New York and London. And Cunard donated a transatlantic passage on the QE2. Now having this complete cruise/fly vacation package of a lifetime I printed tickets for an opportunity drawing and 500 were sold at $10.00 each.

Although the entire event cost was approximately $10,000.00 and we raised $5,000.00 I was able to obtain media cover allowing awareness that will instil public support of preserving the Queen for many years to come.

I wanted the 59th Anniversary launch event to be (1) a celebration of craftsmanship and pride for those who built her, worked on her and celebrated her history, and (2) to be an attraction for those locally to experience what I have known for sometime: That the *Queen Mary* is a world treasure on display in our own front yard.

The planning for this event was everything any event appears to be: fabulous, painful, fun, miserable, detailed, flexible. When it came down to the final day, everything fell into place and the dedication to this project shone through like a ships polished brass bell.

Over and over I was questioned "Why the 59th"? Why not the 60th? I continued to answer "Well, first of all these *Queen Mary* dignitaries are still alive" . Second, the RMS Foundation needs the publicity that would cross the seas to let future guests know we are open and ready for their visit. Lastly, I knew I was probably the only one willing to accept the challenge to make this happen. Sometimes I just had to say "Why the hell not?"

While I was in Clydebank/Glasgow I really enjoyed my 3-night stay over with John Brown. One night while having a "wee dram", Dr. Brown brought out his late wife's diary. He turned to the pages of 1969. He began to read to me the last time he had seen the *Queen Mary*, it was during the retrofit from a 31 year ocean liner to what would be Long Beach's landmark attraction. John read to me names I was familiar with such as "Rados". Rados was the firm that has provided engineering and maritime consulting since the beginning as well as the same company which 25 years later produced the most inaccurate reports ever on the *Queen Mary*'s present condition (which were later disproved by tests and x-rays from 2 other sources, a professional diving company and the U.S. Navy). Rados' reports were obviously slanted in favour of selling, scrapping or sinking the ship. I rather imagine this was because the Port of Long Beach and its Harbor Commission were paying for this study as well as being one of Rados' major contract awarders and supporters over the years.

I still wonder what do the Mayor, Harbor

Commissions and the Port of Long Beach gain if the *Queen Mary* ceases to exist in Long Beach. Its all a mystery to me!

For me, personally and professionally, the *Queen Mary* offers the best in business, travel, pleasure, history and uniqueness. Nowhere else in Long Beach (or probably the world) can you have a 365 sleeping-room hotel, abundant convention and meeting space, a historic and symbolic landmark, a wedding chapel, fine dining, two shopping areas, community college classes, and seasonal fireworks displays, all within a vessel rich in the history of luxury cruising of world ports, movie making and celebrity-catering, and even a bit of public servitude as a WWII troop transport ship.

The catering department is the best I've ever worked with, which in my business is most all of them. It's not often you find an employee, let alone many employees, who really like their jobs. I have found, in discussions with the staff at the *Queen Mary* - and not only the catering department - that they do love their jobs and they don't want to see it end. Many have been working there for quite sometime and as of my last talk with some, they weren't actively seeking other employment. It seems that they see the Queen as an institution, a big part of themselves and a big part of their community.

I learned many interesting things in Clydebank about the *Queen Mary* and the people who built her. As Provost Alistair Mcdonald would say, "Clyde Built Is Well Built!"

Once I saw the pride of the Clyde nothing else seemed to matter except the continuing preservation of the *Queen Mary*.

Once I had gathered everyone from Glasgow to Gatwick and we met with you, Mr.Winter, and your wonderful family, we were all now a complete group.

Ron, you were the one *Queen Mary* dignitary I most often corresponded with (usually by fax). You had the most valuable recollection and transatlantic experiences to share. Especially because these were pre-WWII years. This truly is the Art Deco time period which is much sought after in the "here and now". Ron, during our presentations to the *Queen Mary* staff and the participants of the 59th Anniversary Launch event, you relayed

how life was aboard the ship. That too was invaluable because most of us can only imagine and research in books or recreate from archival documenting. Before your sharing, many celebrated the legend of the *Queen Mary* vicariously through pictures and other period memorabilia.

I do wish we could have better utilised your expertise and willingness to donate your time and energy. Actually, I pretty well used a lot of your energies, and I wore myself out too. I still can't get over how much you and Tony look and act alike.

My dreams for the future are many. I would like the 26th September 1994 for the Sixtieth anniversary celebrations to be a few days long (Friday 23rd - Monday 26th). Perhaps to include the Clydebank - Long Beach Sister City formalisation. The Clydebank display area in place on the ship. John Brown's instruments proudly displayed. The opportunity to meet others who have dedicated some part of themselves to this ship I call indestructible.

Other than Mr. Prevratil I am probably the only one who gets to try to balance all the sides of the *Queen Mary* saga. Preservation vs. restoration vs. revenue. Negative publicity vs. positive daily revelations. It can be difficult but always worth it! What keeps the dream alive for the *Queen Mary* is what keeps each of us thinking in an often unkind world is its potential for opportunity.

The *Queen Mary* remains the positive image of Long Beach and California. Around the world it's known for opulence, elegance and grandeur. I'm working to protect and preserve that.

Everyone should have the opportunity to experience the one of a kind *Queen Mary*. The people of Long Beach are proud of the Queen. I in particular love to show off my Queen. Everyone deserves the right to be proud of our landmark.

The *Queen Mary* and the Atlantic Ocean survived a 31 year marriage. The Queen and the City of Long Beach have been joined for 26 years. Its been good and bad, steady and turbulent. But most of all, it's been "consistently inconsistent".

Long Live The *Queen Mary* In Long Beach.

Chapter 23

Functional Restoration of the Queen Mary

by William E. Cwiklo

William E. Cwiklo is a businessman, a nationally known legal automation consultant and writer. A life-long ship aficionado, he had the good fortune to live aboard the Queen Mary for months at a time in the early 1980's while commuting between Washington, D.C. and Los Angeles on business. The Queen Mary became his home away from home for more than a decade.

A student of the applied arts and inveterate traveller, he was puzzled and disappointed the first time he visited the ship. Aided by a copy of the original Shipbuilder's Engineering Number published at the time of her maiden voyage, he realised that the shortcomings of his hotel and tourist experience were the result of ill-considered "conversion" done between 1968-71 and perpetuated by the taste and predilections of various managers.

As a result of his experience, he has been a strong and vocal advocate of a more respectful treatment with more functional restoration of the ship.

Winston Churchill, a frequent passenger on the *Queen Mary*, is quoted as saying, "You can always count on Americans to do the right thing - after they have exhausted every other possibility." Hopefully, his insight into the American character bodes well for the future history of the *Queen Mary* in Long Beach, California.

The ship that sailed into Long Beach Harbor on 9th December, 1967 was saved from the breakers by the citizens and tideland oil revenues of this fine city. While she bore the wear and tear of 31 years of continual service (and as many layers of paint) she was essentially the same ship that C.W.R. Winter described so vividly in his book, "Queen Mary, Her Early Years." She incorporated three full service hotels within the

structure of one of the most spectacular works of naval architecture and naval engineering of the twentieth century. Her fabulous interior decor, while in need of some restoration, was essentially intact.

What followed was a conversion to shoreside attraction that unwittingly seems to have been inspired by the fate of the *Great Eastern*. Towards the end of her career, this spectacular 19th century ship was docked off Liverpool and opened to the public as a fun fair.

The conversion undermined the inherent historical, architectural and artistic value of the *Queen Mary*, its prime attraction values. The result of the costly remodelling of the *Queen Mary* commissioned by the City of Long Beach and completed between 1968 and 1971 was a ship (technically a floating building) that resembled a second class steamer docked at an amusement park, more than it resembled the legendary RMS *Queen Mary* in port.

Because of the ill-conceived conversion and the high maintenance costs of the facility, all of the operators have had to wrestle with enormous financial burdens just to keep the ship open. Since their backgrounds have been in the amusement park business, and not in the historic attraction area, their approach to increasing revenues is not surprising. It has been to add more catering facilities for meetings and banquets, more souvenir shops and more fast food facilities for tourists in ever more conspicuous locations. Their planning focus has been on short term financial gain.

A common complaint from both tourists and hotel guests today is that there is not enough of interest aboard the ship for tourists to see or for hotel guests to do. One reason for these complaints is that too much functionality was stripped out during the conversion. For example:

• The entire power plant, a marvel of twentieth century mechanical engineering, including the propulsion system, energy plant for ship/hotel services, the forward engine room and all boilers were gutted to make room for a failed Cousteau "Living Sea Museum", a never built "Museum of the Sea" - and for the scrap value of the copper tubing!

• While a hotel was carved out of the first class cabin decks during the 1968-71 conversion, key amenities that would have allowed the ship to function as a premier destination resort hotel such as the two gymnasiums, three barber/beauty salons, two swimming pools, and turkish baths, were either completely gutted or made unsafe to operate.

• When the ship was opened in 1971, management decided to requisition all of the great public rooms on the upper decks for meeting/banqueting services, rather than complete the refurbishment of the existing dining rooms and add new ones on R Deck as was originally intended. As a result, all of the elegant lounges on Promenade and Main Decks were stripped of their furnishings and taken over as catering "ballrooms." Their adjoining areas, once interesting and beautiful spaces in and of themselves, have been harshly treated as storage spaces and pantries.

• The retail outlets installed aboard the ship over the years have varied but the coffee mug and tee shirt variety predominate. Most have no relationship to the original function of the room they occupy, nor are they strongly tied to the ship thematically.

• The Verandah Grill, once the premier a la carte restaurant and nightclub on the North Atlantic had been gutted to make room for a fast food facility. Oddly, old engineer's quarters of no particular architectural or design interest (but with a great view) directly above the Verandah Grill were extensively and expansively rebuilt to house a new restaurant.

Looking Towards the Future

If the *Queen Mary* is to achieve her true post-sailing potential a decisive break with the amusement park approach to her management and operation is required. More than an ambitious advertising campaign, new carpet, new paint, and tighter fiscal controls are required to assure the survival of the RMS *Queen Mary*. A fundamental rethinking of the way the ship is used, the way functions are assigned on board the ship, and the way she is presented to the public is overdue. A rethinking of the role played by the adjoining property is also essential, since they work in concert.

I am convinced that commercial and museum functions can co-exist on the ship with much more original functionality than was ever thought possible.

Functional restoration is the one way to correct many of the problems with the conversion and the current attraction. By functional restoration I mean assigning original or closely related functions to rooms and spaces that reflect the intent of the ship's designers whenever possible.

Fortunately, many original artefacts remain in storage and plans along with an abundance of photographs of the ship as she looked at her most glorious still exist.

The functional restorations discussed herein require no *major* structural changes to the ship. They use original facilities largely as intended. There is enough original furniture in storage or scattered about the ship to refurnish many original areas. Some examples of original functionality remain.

1. The Observation Bar looks, feels and functions much like it did when the ship was in service. The furniture and colour scheme are not original, but this could easily be put right.

2. The first class restaurant (now called the Grand Salon) hosts the Sunday Brunch that captures some of the visual and culinary excitement that were found here when this room served as the main dining room for first class passengers.

3. Most cabins on the hotel decks are original first class cabins, modified in only minor ways.

Other functional restorations could be achieved quite easily. For instance one could:

• Put out deck chairs for use with beverage service on Promenade Deck (and on Sun Deck in good weather). Deck chairs weren't free with passage when the ship was in service. They needn't be free now either. Use them in conjunction with attended bar service or rent them by the hour.

• Use some of the acres of deck space for deck games with an appropriate hourly rental.

• Re-install the original first class gymnasium as a display and interpretative area.

• Offer entertainment in the public areas of the ship which reflects the heyday of the *Queen Mary*.

• Remove the tee-shirt shops, gewgaw stalls and penny press machines found and replace them with discretely located and well-designed revenue generating features that reflect the golden age of travel, such as:
- an international newspaper stand (a boon for those using the deck chairs);
- shoe-shine stand;
- a fresh flower stall; and
- steward assisted beverage service utilising deck chairs.

• Create a set of interpretative shops in Prom Deck Square that enhance the *Queen Mary* experience. Interpretative shops, as opposed to leased gift shops, involve curatorial staff in the buying, displaying and selling of merchandise. For example:
- A good book store in the first class library.
- A children's toy store in the first class children's playroom would be wonderful.
- Instead of using the first class writing room as a ladies lavatory, why not restore the writing room as an interpretative area and use it to sell RMS *Queen Mary* stationary, notes, writing instruments and so on. Here visitors might pause to buy and write a note, fill out their ship questionnaire, give us their address for our mailing list and have letters posted from the *Queen Mary*.

• Instead of scattering vintage English telephone booths on the Sun Deck, (where they surely would have been blown off in the first North Atlantic gale), I suggest using the first class passenger Radio Telephone Room on Promenade Deck as a public telephone area and a place where one could send faxes from the *Queen Mary*.

• Instead of using the first class lecture room on Promenade Deck to sell tee shirts, I suggest using it to offer the opening presentation for a guided tour on the Art Deco heritage of the *Queen Mary*.

In this way, commercial use and interpretative experience become so closely linked. Hopefully, visitors will get a much better sense of what it was like to be a passenger. This will likely encourage visitors to spend more time (and money) aboard the ship.

The area that needs attention first is Promenade Deck. Promenade Deck was and still is the most public deck of the *Queen Mary*. Here were and are located most of the major public lounges, shops and bars. It is here that we must convince the public that the *Queen Mary* is special. Given the frequent turnover of shops in Prom Deck Square (three different merchants have occupied the center shop, originally an Austin Reed shop, in the last 12 months), there seems to be little risk in trying a retailing strategy that ties the shop more closely to their original functions of these rooms.

Museum Displays and Tours

To understand how original artefacts are displayed on the *Queen Mary* of today you need to think of the *Queen Mary* as a gigantic cocktail shaker. Everything that wasn't nailed down has been moved so often that it is only in its original location by the purest of chance. The curatorial concept of displaying objects "in situ", that is in their original location, has been disregarded.

The worst culprit in this scenario is the "ship walk." The ship walk is a self-guided path through the upper decks designed to move 10,000 to 12,000 paying tourists through the ship each day. However, the ship cannot comfortably handle that many people at once, nor can people be allowed to wander at will through the hotel decks. So a "ship walk" was designed to shepherd tourists on a pre-digested route of displays on the upper decks and in a restricted area in the stern — and to keep them moving.

A key feature of the ship walk is displays of original artefacts removed from elsewhere on the ship. Thus, there is a "First Class Drawing Room" display in a former funnel hatch - even though the real first class drawing room is one deck below occupied by a tee shirt and coffee mug variety of souvenir store. There is also a mock-up of a corner of the first class children's playroom - even though the real thing is also just one deck below — used to sell coffee and candy.

• An exhibit on Sun Deck includes a number of artefacts from the ship's synagogue - a unique facility that was the first built into a ship. Much of the original panelling is available in storage. The single-guided tour walks right past the site of the synagogue and the site is pointed out by the tour guide, - even though the room is totally empty and not being used.

• Likewise the Third Class Children's Playroom sits empty and locked nearby though its fittings are still stored aboard the ship.

• The Second Class Library is being misused as a banqueting stack chair storage space even though most of its fixtures are still on the ship and the guided tour passes right by. It could be viewed on a guided tour and

would make a nice amenity for use by hotel guests.

Instead of the ship walk, I suggest the development of a series of guided tours that highlight the three main facets of the ship. These are: 1) the passenger areas, 2) the crew and working areas, and 3) the navigational and engineering aspects of the ship. They lend themselves to three quite different and unique tour routes. All of the artefacts on the ship walk could be returned to their original (or close to original) locations and used as exhibits "in situ" on guided tours. Assisted by an admission policy that encourages the taking of guided tours, revenues could rise significantly.

Hearst Castle as an Example

Hearst Castle is the most successful historic tourist attraction in California. It has a program of three guided tours, plus a night tour that includes highlights from the three daytime tours, and includes a reception.

Each of the three daytime tours at Hearst's Castle cost more than twice the amount charged for the single tour on the *Queen Mary* and they are so popular that advanced reservations are required. The night tour costs $25 per person. Reservations are required weeks in advance for the night tour because of demand.

Could it be because the functional, artistic, decorative and historic aspects of Hearst's Castle have been preserved and are intact?

It is interesting to note that Hearst's Castle is a vast old pile of a house located a long drive (250 miles north of Los Angeles and 250 mile south of San Francisco) from major population areas. It has high maintenance costs and was left no endowment. Operated by the State of California, it is successful enough to run in the black and in good years generates enough surplus revenue to support half of the state's other museums. Paid attendance figures for Hearst Castle and the *Queen Mary* are similar - about 1,000,000 people per year.

Not even a cup of tea is served to daytime tourists on the hill top. The tee shirts and fast food facilities that line the public decks of the *Queen Mary* are nowhere to be seen up on the hill at Heast's Castle. Just as at Colonial Williamsburg, they are restricted to a visitor's information center - which at Hearst Castle is located at the bottom of the hill, miles down hill from the house.

The Hotel Queen Mary

The RMS *Queen Mary* that sailed into long Beach contained three full service hotels with a vast array of resort amenities including two gymnasiums, two indoor swimming pools, acres of deck for sports, recreation and relaxation, a Turkish bath, multiple barber shops and beauty salon facilities, numerous lounges, bars and restaurants where passengers could wile away the hours during a crossing.

Today's Hotel *Queen Mary* offers you a small but interesting room (most often in an original first class cabin) and good meeting/banqueting services [1]. There is no longer a working swimming pool, nor a gymnasium or fitness center, and just a small lounge by the registration desk that is reserved for hotel guests use. On the upper decks there are two public bars, three public restaurants, numerous fast food facilities, shops and a guided tour.

The absence of standard first class hotel amenities and recreational facilities is the result of decisions made by early operators of the ship in Long Beach. They decided to target the meeting/conference market. They felt that the resort amenities were too expensive to maintain and in the way of catering services. Over time, they were gutted (to little or no financial advantage) as being of no interest whatsoever.

Fortunately, many of the furnishings remain aboard the ship. And the rooms in which they were located, while requisitioned for various housekeeping functions, could be made available for functional restoration.

The Travel Bureau -
an example of functional restoration

Pacifica Travel has maintained a travel service facility aboard the ship for hotel guests for the past 10 years. Located in a cabin on A deck, in recent months business requirement necessitated more space. The curator suggested installing them in the original First Class Travel Bureau on Main Deck.

Once the decision was made several original pieces of furniture from this room were identified aboard the ship. By swapping, begging and barter they were made available for the restored travel bureau. The ship's furniture workshop reupholstered two original chairs. A ship aficionado and craftsman was

found to change the electronic engines in the original fans for their use with American electrical current.

It is not complete yet. The large stylised wall map from the back of the room is still in the museum. Since the back wall has a door through the center that is used to access the back work room (originally this work area wasn't part of the travel bureau, but was two inside cabins) a decision is pending from Pacifica on whether they prefer historic and artistic integrity over convenience.

Putting the travel bureau back together for functional use in its original location was neither difficult nor costly. It simply took determination on the part of the curator and Pacifica Travel and the support of the CEO. This is the first functional restoration of the RMS Foundation since assuming operational control in February of 1993.

Other functional restoration projects on the ship that might appeal to hotel guests include:

• A Health Spa in the former first class pool and Turkish bath area and linked by elevator to...

• A fitness center on Sun Deck where the first class gymnasium and squash courts were located (now a fast food outlet) and the adjoining Sports deck where the first class triple deck tennis courts were located - now occupied by unused fast food stalls and air conditioning equipment that should have been fitted in the funnels.

• The first class barber and beauty salons in their original locations on B deck - perfectly situated for spa guest use. They were dismantled and the space is now used for cash control.

• A hotel guest only lounge and entertainment center at the back of Main Deck in the original Second Class Main Lounge.

• An indoor/outdoor restaurant and nightclub in the Verandah Grill, once the premier a la carte restaurant and night club on the North Atlantic - now sadly, a fast food outlet.

Catering and the Upper Decks

Catering, that is hosting private special events such as dinners, dances, weddings and meetings is probably the largest source of revenue on the *Queen Mary*. The services

---

1 The average hotel room on the *Queen Mary* is 200 square feet. The average hotel room in most contemporary first class hotels is 400 square feet.

provided are professional and well done. Unfortunately, they monopolise all of the major public rooms on the ship. By rethinking how one sells and holds functions on the ship, it might be possible to increase revenues and create a more unique shipboard experience.

Today, all major public rooms are stripped and reserved for catering functions. These might require that a room be set up with tables and chairs for a sit-down-dinner, or for an event that requires rows of chairs set up theatre style, a business meeting, a seminar requiring a "school room" setting, or a large dance that requires an essentially bare room.

The result of these varied needs is that much of the original furniture in these fabulous public rooms is in storage - or was sold off by the city. These rooms take a beating from constant setting-up and taking down of metal stack chairs and tables. Moreover, large adjoining areas suffer severe damage to the original woodwork and light fixtures because they are used as storage spaces or were gutted for pantries. Finally, the constant take down and set up is labor intensive and costly.

One alternative would be to sell elegant receptions and dinners held in two rooms rather than per plate dinner/dances jammed into a single room.

By this I mean, start with a cocktail and reception in an original lounge on the upper decks, then lead guests down one of the ship's grand staircases to dinner on R deck in an original dining room.

This would allow catering guests to see more of the ship, provide a better impression and allow restoration of the upper deck lounges as reception rooms. Many of their original furnishings remain aboard the ship. Using the original dining rooms on R. Deck for dining makes sense because the ship's main kitchens remain on this deck. Adding dining rooms aft would be simple since all of the second class cabins and stewards quarters located here were completely gutted twenty five years ago.

Much of the damage to the ship associated with the setting up and removal of furniture could be eliminated as would the costly labor. R Deck dining rooms could be refurnished with "real" chairs as opposed to banqueting stack chairs. And the need for all the storage space would disappear.

While this might appear to limit the number of receptions held at one time, all of the rooms are never booked at once - except possibly on New Years Eve. The higher quality of the experience and service would mean the operator could charge a higher price for the service.

Rooms for business meetings requiring state of the art audio visual equipment and theatre style set ups and a vast exhibit hall could be built into a new hotel off the ship. I suggest we build an "Ocean Terminal" hotel based on the exterior of Ocean Terminal in Southampton to house this new facility.

The Queen Mary as Naval Architecture and a Work of Engineering

The forward areas (B Deck to G Deck) now closed and used to store the vast supply of original furniture and fittings stripped from the "ballrooms" or simply empty and closed include original crew areas that should be reopened for tours.

These areas are so large that more than tour use is possible.

- A youth hostel in original crew areas that gives young adults of today a brief experience of living in the crew quarters of the 1930's is one possibility. Or perhaps a work study program on restoration might be housed here.

- When the 25 year old power plant for the ship (located three quarters of a mile from the ship and not terribly energy efficient) reaches the end of its useful life, Boiler Room Number 1 remains empty and available to house a new energy plant to supply power and hotwater for the ship.

- The forward holds have ample storage space for the ships stores and supplies. Restoring functionality to the cranes on the bow and lift mechanisms in the holds would permit better access to this area.

- The ship lost its C Deck working alley in 1971 when it was cut away amidship. D Deck still runs the length of the ship and has service entrances forward and aft and thus could be used as a working alley, solving major logistic problems in moving supplies on the ship.

- A guided tour of the bridge and remaining engine room and propeller shaft would be helpful. They are not self-explanatory to most people.

The Adjoining Property

Sorting out functions aboard the ship requires developing a master plan not only for the ship, but also for the adjoining property that works in concert with it.

- The *Queen Mary* had a captive audience of 2,000 to 3,000 people that filled its restaurants, lounges and mess halls. A 395 cabin hotel doesn't supply enough of an audience to support the ship.

A new "Ocean Terminal Hotel" built nearby with 600 additional hotel rooms, new meeting rooms with state of the art audio visual equipment for seminars and business meetings and a large exhibit hall would be a big help. It would allow the *Queen Mary* to host major conferences, while still restoring original amenities aboard the *Queen Mary* for hospitality use.

With more hotel rooms on the property, the cabins on the ship, mostly with an adjoining internal door could be used as bedroom-sitting room mini-suites (with two bathrooms) rather than as cramped singles. Little or no construction would be required. In many cases one would simply need to replace the bed in one room with a sofa bed and add some chairs.

- The former Spruce Goose Dome, if converted into a world class entertainment center would draw large crowds to the ship. Before and after events, the crowds could be invited to use the restaurants, lounges, dance areas and bars on Promenade Deck. The ship could host before and after theatre buffets in the first class dining room. And theatre guests might be inclined to spend the night on the ship or in the proposed Ocean Terminal Hotel.

While various uses of the dome would provide synergy, it is important to select a use that compliments the *Queen Mary*, not one that competes with it, or targets an audience unlikely to appreciate the uniqueness and/or history of the ship.

- An aquarium near the ship would likely encourage a family orientated audience interested in an educational experience during the day.
- The English style village built near the ship

years ago could be an interesting retail experience... if it were comprised of unique British shops, instead of more souvenir shops, tee shirt shops and fast food facilities.

- A marina at the bow for historic sailing ships, and a cruise ship pier at the stern would round out the property nicely.

Summary

It is extremely unlikely that engines will ever again be re-installed in the *Queen Mary* or that she will ever again cross any ocean. And because of her enormous size and equally high maintenance costs the various operators have continually argued that the shop cannot "earn her keep" simply as a historical preservation project. But to succeed as an attraction, the *Queen Mary* must be true to herself. Functional restoration is a means to preserving and restoring the ship as well as making her a viable commercial attraction.

There have always been alternatives. Opportunities for a better functional fit and more accurate presentation arise almost daily. The look and feel of the *Queen Mary* today is the result of the conversion, but it also reflects the tastes, personal agendas and the decisions of the various operators over the past twenty plus years.

Responsibility for the appropriate use of the ship also lies with the owner, the City of Long Beach. After city politicians and bureaucrats were embarrassed by exposés of financial mismanagement during the conversion and early years of operation of the ship they essentially backed away from operations and decision making. Little or no city money has been spent on the ship or property for more than a decade.

Is the *Queen Mary* worth the effort? Again the words of Winston Churchill best summarise the value of the *Queen Mary* to Long Beach and to the world.

"Built for the arts of peace and to link the old world with the new, the Queens challenged the fury of Hitlerism.... to defend the liberties of civilisation. Vital decisions depended on their ability continuously to elude the enemy, and without their aid, the day of final Victory must unquestionably have been postponed. To those who brought these two great ships into existence, the world owes a debt that will not be easy to measure."

Chapter 24

Comments by the Director of Development

by Travis A. Montgomery

During the last 26 years Travis Montgomery has been able to watch the progress of the Queen Mary from several different points of view, and for many of these years he worked for the Port of Long Beach, the Harbour Authority who were responsible for her operation. Today, as Development Director for RMS Foundation Inc., no one is in a better position to influence her future. He is, in a sense, her Navigating Officer, charged with the responsibility of guiding her safely through the uncharted waters of the future. He writes as follows ;

On 9th December, 1967, I was on the thirtieth floor of a high rise building in downtown Long Beach observing the arrival of The *Queen Mary* in Long Beach. Since, I have had the pleasure of participating in many *Queen Mary* firsts, all of which have had a strong impact on our community and me personally.

While the ship was being "refitted" as a tourist attraction, I was privileged to tour her on several occasions during 1968, 1969 and 1970. ~I was also able to go onboard in late December 1967, before any of the work started. The graffiti from the crew of the final sailing was still on the bulkheads during this 1967 visit. This was a statement of the pride that the British felt for The *Queen Mary*, and of the fear that this queen of the seas would not be properly cared for and respected in her new home. It was evident The *Queen Mary* was more than just another ship to her crew.

Throughout the years, as I grew in fond-ness for The *Queen Mary*, I did so as a citizen of the community, not as an employee of the great ship. For eleven years, as an employee of the Port of Long Beach, I was able to participate in such events as the addition of the Spruce Goose to The *Queen Mary* property. On frequent overseas journeys, I learned first hand how inseparable Long Beach and The *Queen Mary* had become. Everywhere I visited, mention The *Queen Mary*, and people would respond Long Beach. Mention Long Beach and the response was *Queen Mary*. During these travels, I would estimate I have given away several thousand *Queen Mary* tie bars promoting our city's great treasure.

In 1993, I became one of the early members of the staff of the RMS Foundation, Inc., which began operation of The *Queen Mary* on 26th February 1993. Since then, I now am part of the process working to share The *Queen Mary* with visitors from throughout the world, and to preserve her great heritage for those in the future to share.

Today, as in the past, The *Queen Mary* and Long Beach are synonymous terms and I am excited to be working to guarantee that this continues. As we celebrate the Sixtieth Anniversary of the launch of The *Queen Mary* this 26th September, 1994, I look forward to many celebrations highlighting the longevity of the great *Queen Mary*.

Chapter 25

Queen Mary: Sailing into the 21st Century

by Joseph F. Prevratil

As the one responsible for the successful operation of the Queen Mary in Long Beach, Joe Prevratil is the man stuck with the buck. His is a fearsome responsibility, and he began his second reign as Supremo in February 1993 with a legacy of failed policies and costly mistakes. But in his first stint in control, under Wrather Port Properties, he demonstrated that he has the ability, and that it is possible to produce a 'bottom line' showing a profit, and at the same time to placate the preservationists.
There are a number of people watching his progress with great interest, anxious to help in any way possible, and among these I humbly number myself.

Historic tourism is one of the fastest growing industries worldwide. The *Queen Mary* offers a unique blend of qualities which attract this patronage. In recent decades, Long Beach has competed successfully with Los Angeles and Orange County as a cultural center and destination for tourists. This trend combined with the innate worth of the *Queen Mary* gives her a distinct marketing advantage. Many tourists are more attracted to authenticity than contrived amusements and are willing to pay more for the experience.

Traditionally, the general attraction, catering and hotel facilities generated most of the revenue, but now we have the option of tapping resources never before explored. We plan to embark on a restoration project that will create a more interactional experience for *Queen Mary* guests and will duplicate many of the amenities enjoyed by passengers who travelled aboard her on an Atlantic crossing. The first class swimming pool on

"R" deck is a high priority in this renovation, along with the Verandah Grill and Long Gallery on the Sun and Promenade decks.

Long Beach, now a city with a population of nearly half a million, was originally a Navy and shipbuilding community with no distinctive identity. The early city-planners searched for something to highlight their maritime history and to create the image of a waterfront resort. The rejuvenation of Long Beach is largely due to the presence of the *Queen Mary* which has given the city a symbol of which to be proud. According to research conducted by the Long Beach area Convention and Visitor's Council, 1 out of 3 visitors to the city cite the *Queen Mary* as their principal destination.

At first, I was not considering taking over the management of the *Queen Mary* when the Disney Company left, but certain factors indicated the appropriateness of this decision. I had experience in the operation of the vessel under Wrather Port Properties, as well as public support for my new proposal to keep and run the *Queen Mary* in Long Beach. The transition would be less complicated with a trained staff already on hand.

The ship's employees were among my most loyal proponents, together with business owners and preservationist groups such as the Merchant Marine Veterans of World War II and The *Queen Mary* Foundation. I believe in investing in people and this policy has cultivated a positive relationship between employees, merchants and volunteer preservationists. These people, like a ship's crew, are the life of the ship and they will make the best of the *Queen Mary*'s vast potential.

The summer festivities were officially begun with the grand opening on 23rd June 1993. In the first five weeks after this event, 261,551 people had come to visit the *Queen Mary*. On the Fourth of July weekend alone we registered a total of 62,000.

Initially, I charged no admission fee, expecting that this might generate interest in the *Queen Mary*, even among people who had never visited her before. The large numbers who visited the ship soon made the introduction of a five dollar charge seem justified. Visitors or guests have the option of joining our "Captain's Club" for one low annual fee. This entitles members to free parking and admission, as well as a quarterly newsletter announcing upcoming attractions.

We look forward to a new era in the *Queen Mary*'s career. Several new projects and special events are currently in the planning stages.

The *Queen Mary* essentially comprises two different types of attraction: her historic significance and the holding of special events on board in her 25,000sf exhibit hall. Our goal is to have at least one major event each month. The 60th Anniversary of the *Queen Mary*'s launch promises to be one of the most important dates in the history of the ship.

There is a market for quality *Queen Mary* merchandise as well as for traditional souvenirs. We are exploring the possibility of having reproductions made of the *Queen Mary*'s popular Art-Deco style furniture and lamp fixtures and offering them for sale. This would enable the serious enthusiast to carry away more than just a fond memory.

Commercial and preservationist interests, by working together, can guarantee profit for the *Queen Mary*. It is my belief that, in this case, historic preservation and financial viability will go hand-in-hand. In this the sixtieth year since the *Queen Mary*'s construction, we look forward to a successful future for her as she heads into the twenty-first century.

Chapter 26

Her Maritime Majesty

It was Hal Johnson who dreamed up the above title for the *Queen Mary*, and like so many other American slogans, it hits the metaphorical nail fair and square on its head. If you read what Hal has written about the ship you will realise that here is a man, a practical marine surveyor and diver, who has an abiding love for all ships, and for this one in particular. And Hal is not alone in this by any means. Read what the others have said; George Kean, another very practical engineer, Diane Rush and David Rubin, both of whom devote a major part of their lives to serving the Queen, David Hutchings, who is a well known author with books about this and other ships to his name. And there are many more, hundreds of us, even thousands of us, throughout the world who feel the same way.

Why do we love ships? Is it because they enable us to cope with what is after all a hostile and dangerous element, the sea, and one that man was not designed to live in, nor to travel great distances in? Is it because they make us feel superior and the master of nature? If the latter, then we deceive ourselves, for man is a puny animal and nature is all powerful. Deep water sailors learn this very quickly, and the North Atlantic is an excellent school. But perhaps it is easier out there, against the

awful splendour of that immense backdrop of sky and sea, to put things in perspective, to remember God's presence and our own insignificance. But when you are out there remember it you do, and daily give thanks for your continued preservation.

In an earlier chapter I posed the question as to why men go to sea when the disadvantages and discomforts are so great, and I have tried to suggest some of the reasons. Perhaps I should have emphasised this relationship with nature for there is something fundamental in your utter dependence on the ship you are in, for it is all that stands between you and a watery grave. I believe that all sailors recognise this, though perhaps subconsciously.

But there must be some additional quality about the *Queen Mary* that makes her so universally popular, for many of her adherents and staunchest supporters are not sailors, and indeed the majority today were not even alive when she first went into service in 1936. What is this elusive characteristic which unites us all in the service of this huge example of man's ingenuity and engineering skill? Surely it must be that she has a personality, something intangible, a thing of the spirit, but all her own. Diane Rush has said this, George Kean has said it - he has called her 'the ship

with a soul' - and I think we all feel it. It is a powerful force that cannot be quantified in terms of profit and loss.

Memories keep flooding back, old memo-

Top: *Off Cowes, Isle of Wight, inward bound.* (David F. Hutchings).

Above: *Getting ready to depart on yet another transatlantic voyage.*

The actual telegraph with which the Staff Chief stopped the ship.
(University Archives, University of Liverpool).

ries of the time I spent in her when she was new and the eighth wonder of the world, and these have now been joined by new memories of her 59th birthday in 1993 and the

"DANG!"

blissful week I spent aboard her then. Earlier in this book I devoted a whole chapter to memories, and at the risk of boring you I must share a few more with you. Some are good, and some are not so good, as for example the remembrance of the terror experienced by passengers when she was rolling badly. This was distressing to see, and for me it was the first time in my life that I had witnessed human beings stripped of their veneer of civilisation and drooling with fear like animals.

But among the good memories, for example, is the joy I experienced in looking out of a porthole way up forward in the bows where I was above the bow wave. If you did this at dawn then the great fountain of water below you was filled with all the colours of the rainbow, and it was pure magic. As you may imagine it was not often possible to do this, for you had to be on the 4-8 watch in the Forward Generating Room, for then one of your duties was to inspect the Chernikeef Log in its little compartment up forward on the port side.

Those watches spent on the Switchboards on either generating station were excessively boring, for when the turbo-generators were running sweetly, and as long as you kept an eye on your instruments and filled in the log hourly there was absolutely nothing to do, no mental activity at all. So I was driven to invent my own means of keeping my brain active, and started writing poetry and short stories, and designing beautiful houses to live in. None of which was any good, but it did pass many a frustrating hour away.

Mind you, when things did go wrong there was plenty to do, but this did not happen often, for all the machinery and equipment in the *Queen Mary* was of the highest possible quality, the very best of British engineering practice. Indeed it was only human error that caused any hiccough in the sweet running of the plant, as for example when the Staff Chief Engineer on one of his infrequent visits to the Engine Room gave a foolish order which very nearly shut the whole ship down. The story is told in my previous book "Queen Mary: Her Early Years Recalled", but as it is a good one I will recount it again.

It occurred at the beginning of one eastward voyage when we were outward bound from New York. We dropped the pilot as usual as we passed the Ambrose Light

Vessel, and then it was full speed ahead for home. As the ship gathered speed all the electrical auxiliaries, circulating pumps, boiler feed pumps, etc., etc., had to be speeded up and the electrical load rose rapidly. This was expected, and to cope with it it was necessary to have a spare turbo-generator running in plenty of time, and we always did this.

On the forward engine room starting platform there was a telegraph connected with the after generating room, and this indicated how many generators were running and the load they were carrying. The Staff Chief, who should have known better, saw that there was one generator without any load on it, so he rang through on the telegraph "Shut down one generator". The engineer on the switchboard was in a quandary, for he knew that very soon the load would start its rapid rise, so he rang the forward engine room to ask for confirmation. He got it, and a flea in his ear, from the Staff Chief who told him to do as he was told. So he shut down the spare generator.

Then things started to happen. The bridge rang down "full speed ahead" and the electrical load started its inevitable rise. Soon the two generators that were running could not cope with the load. To prevent damage to them it was automatic that in the event of overload certain circuits should trip out, and this now took place. Unfortunately these circuits had never been checked, and no one realised that by mistake the one that fed the boiler feed pumps had been included. So these pumps stopped and the supply of water to the boilers stopped too, the steam pressure dropped, the turbo-generators slowed down, the voltage of the power they were producing dropped and more circuits tripped out.

The ship came to a standstill, all the lights went out in the passenger accommodation, and for a few minutes it looked as through a complete shutdown was inevitable. Fortunately this was avoided but we reached a situation where there was only enough steam to run one generator on the hotel services switchboard. The two switchboards were quickly linked together and very slowly the load was built up again. I can vouch for this for I was the engineer on the switchboard at the time.

The incident gave the junior engineers much amusement, for the Staff Chief was a bumptious and self-important little man, and

A matter of scale!

we would love to have heard the inevitable ticking-off he received from the Chief. His immediate excuse at the time was that he leaned accidentally on the telegraph, but this was nonsense for the telegraph was so positioned that it was quite impossible for anyone to lean on it. Incidentally, this actual telegraph is now on display in the *Queen Mary*'s Exhibition Room.

Another little incident I remember was recounted to me by an engineer who had previously served in the *Berengaria*. She was a German built ship, the *Imperator,* handed over to Cunard in 1919 as part of their war reparations. She was apparently in good running order, but was full of cunning

Above: *Swinging her into position for the last time in Southampton.* (University Archives, University of Liverpool).
Left: *Captain John Treasure Jones, her last Skipper.* (David F. Hutchings).

little booby traps. One of these was on the main steam line between boiler rooms and engine room, and it took a little finding. A flanged joint between two lengths of pipe had been unbolted and a thin plate inserted, solid but for a small hole in the centre. When steam was raised to get the ship under way, the gauge on the engine room starting platform showed the correct pressure, but when the valve was opened to let steam into the turbine nothing happened, for the plate which the Germans had inserted was a baffle and only a very small volume of steam could get through the small hole. Difficult to find, but easy to correct once found.

Sounds that I shall always remember from those far-off days include the clanging of the warning bells as the watertight doors were shutting. And another sound was the steady drone of the caller's voice on one voyage when we carried members of the American Legion to Europe for a tour of the first world war battlefields, and a bunch of enterprising stewards ran a continuous school of 'housey-housey', 24 hours a day. Also the haunting sound of a party of American College students singing 'Santa Lucia' and other student songs one almost tropical night in mid Atlantic. Nor will I ever forget the heart-breaking gypsy melodies played on a violin on the foredeck one night when the third class accommodation was full of Austrian refugees fleeing from Hitler after the Anschluss.

In lighter mood I smile when I remember the practical jokes we younger engineers played on each other, but even this memory brings in sad thoughts, for my great friend John Rennie, who was party to many of these tricks, is no longer with us. John was a bit gullible, and was often the butt of jokes himself, indeed we all suffered from time to time. One morning John was cleaning out the goldfish tank in his cabin - most of us kept a few goldfish on our writing desks - and a number of his friends were watching him, and perhaps waiting for any opportunity that might arise. He carefully put the plug in his washbasin and emptied the water and fish into it while he wiped out the tank. While he was busy with this we managed to transfer the fish into another container, and as John turned round to fetch them from the washbasin we pulled out the plug. The timing was perfect, he saw the last of the water running out, and was convinced the fish had gone too. For a few moments he was furious, until he realised that the fish were safe, and that he had been had.

There was much fun in the *Queen Mary* in those early days, and though we all grumbled at the long hours and hard work, there was a good spirit in the ship, and we were happy.

To those old memories I can now add many others after visiting the ship in 1993. Including the extraordinary feeling of going aboard her in Long Beach after a gap of 55 years, but this time not to go to sea, but to have my heart strings pulled this way and

that, and to try and adjust to all the inevitable changes that have been made. And at this point I must congratulate Joe Prevratil, the present operator, who has an almost impossible task of rescuing her from years of unfortunate policies. There are signs, however, that he understands, better than any of his predecessors, what has to be done, and that her future lies in treating her as a ship - and one with a soul at that - and not just as a building. But perhaps he needs to be persuaded that restoration and conservation can, and indeed must, be part of his management policy, and that they can go hand in hand with profit making. Does he also need to be persuaded that there are many, many people not on his payroll who are willing, able, and indeed eager to help him achieve his material goal, a healthy 'bottom line'? The sooner he can be convinced of this, the sooner his goal will be reached.

His hotel and catering operations are excellent, both of them first class. *Queen Mary* food was always world famous, and it is still in that category, though inevitably now American in character and not European. Criticism has been levelled at the size of some of the cabins, but it must be remembered that she is not a modern custom built hotel, but a 60 year old ship. At the time she was built, passengers in many another Atlantic liner were still sleeping in tiered bunks. It is also possible to criticise the choice of carpets, curtains, furnishing fabrics and light fittings. American attempts to capture authentic British 1930's style are not always completely successful, and it is to be hoped that when these items become due for replacement - though at present day inflated prices long may it be delayed - expert British advice will be sought.

In Chapter 9 I put forward a plea for unity of purpose, and for an inspirational lead that will be the first step towards achieving this. In my view this is indeed the first step in any plans for restoration, for a combination of forces is many times stronger than its individual components - remember the parable of the man who had six sons. So my final plea is to emphasise this, and to urge everyone involved to agree on a policy and then work together in harmony to achieve it. While we squabble and argue amongst ourselves time is slipping away, energies are being dissipated, and Her Maritime Majesty is not getting any younger.

The Management of the ship is naturally motivated by the urge to achieve material success, the *Queen Mary* Foundation is motivated by love of the ship, and a compulsive desire to help, and the City Council is motivated by the knowledge that the *Queen Mary* is a magnet situated at the heart of their tourist industry. In addition to these three major forces there are thousands of ordinary people throughout the world who are motivated by their affectionate regard for the ship and her astonishing achievements over the last 60 years. Let this year of her Diamond Jubilee be the turning point in her career when all the above forces join together with the common aim of making her future equally as illustrious as her past. I make no apology for re-quoting the words of those old English leather workers who 200 years ago realised that unity was strength.

Let us conduct ourselves in all matters of importance
with judgement, coolness and deliberation.

Let everyone lay aside his own private interest
and study the good of the whole.

And lastly, let us study friendship and unanimity
with one another, this will cement our structure and
render it permanent.

Make us the joy of the present and the praise of ages
to come.

Long Live the *Queen Mary*.

Appendix I
The Queen Mary's Career Dates

1930	December 1st	Contract placed with John Brown & Co. Ltd. to build the ship.
1931	December 10	Work suspended
1934	April 3	Work resumed
	September 26	Launched by H.M. Queen Mary in presence of H.M. King George V.
1936	March 24	Left Clydebank for 'the Tail of the Bank' Gourock.
	March 25	Left Gourock for Southampton.
	March 27	Entered King George V Graving Dock.
	April 15	Left Southampton for the Clyde, and Trials.
	April 17	Arrived and anchored off Gourock.
	April 18	Trials, including speed trials off the Isle of Arran. Culminating in 24 hour full speed fuel consumption trial in the Irish Sea.
	May 12	Ship officially handed over by John Brown & Co. Ltd. to Cunard White Star Ltd.
	May 14	Inaugural 24 hour cruise with VIP passengers.
	May 25	Ship visited by King Edward VIII, Queen Mary, and other members of the Royal Family.
	May 27	Voyage No. 1 Maiden Voyage from Southampton to Cherbourg and New York.
	July 22	First Record westward crossing. 3098 nautical miles in 4 days 8 hours 37 minutes. Average speed 29.61 knots. Later broken by *Normandie.*
	August 19-31	Voyage No. 6. Double Record Voyage in both directions. Average speed (westward) 30.01 knots. Average speed (eastward) 30.57 knots.
1937		*Normandie* again recaptured the Blue Riband.
1938	August 10-14	Another record voyage, winning the Blue Riband which she kept for 14 years, finally losing it to the United States in 1952.
1939	September 3	War declared. *Queen Mary* at sea nearing New York.
	September 4	Arrived New York and was immediately laid up.
1940	March 21	Left New York for Sydney for conversion to troopship.
	May 5	Left Sydney for the Clyde with 5000 Australian troops aboard.
	June 16	Arrived Gourock.
	June 29	Left Gourock for Singapore.
	August 5	Arrived Singapore, and into dry dock for 6 week refit.
	September	Left Singapore for Sydney.
	September 25	Arrived Sydney for further alterations to increase troop carrying capacity. Spent the rest of the year trooping.
1941	April	Joined in Sydney by *Queen Elizabeth.* Trooping included 8000 New Zealand soldiers to Egypt, returning with Italian POW's.
	December 19	*Queen Mary* left Sydney for New York.
1942	January 12	Arrived New York.

	January 25	Left New York for Boston Navy Yard for 13 week refit.
	February 18	Left New York for Sydney with total ship's company of 9300. Japanese Radio later reported she had been sunk.
	March 28	Arrived Sydney.
	April 6	Left Sydney for New York to become a North Atlantic G.I. shuttle.
	May 16	Transported nearly 10,000 troops to Gourock. Plan then changed due to Rommel's attack on Egypt from Lybia. Rushed to Port Said with over 9000 troops and military - her longest port to port non-stop passage of 6200 miles under appalling conditions of heat.
	June 23	Sailed for New York with Allied personnel and German POW's.
	July 31	Arrived New York.
	August 2	Sailed for the Clyde with 15,125 troops, the first trip of a regular shuttle service.
	October 2	Tragic Collision with *H.M.S. Curacoa,* with the loss of 331 lives.
	December 23	Taken off shuttle service. Left Gourock for Suez with over 10,000 troops.
1943	January 25	Sailed from Suez for Massawa and Sydney.
	March	Sailed for Gourock with Allied personnel and over 4000 Italian POw's.
	May 5	Left Gourock for New York with over 4000 German POW's.
	June 1	Resumption of transatlantic troop carrying, which continued for next 15 months. The only break in this routine was in August 1943 and again in September 1944 when Winston Churchill crossed in her. On one trip she carried 16,683 persons, the largest number ever accommodated in a ship.
1945	June 15	Sailed from Gourock to New York with almost 15,000 returning G.I.'s.
	August 12	Visited Southampton, her home port, for the first time in 6 years. Continued repatriating runs (with *Queen Elizabeth*)
1946		*Queen Mary* used to repatriate war brides to the United States. In all she carried 12,886 brides, 1683 children, and 2085 infants.
	September 29	Arrived Southampton, completing her war service, having travelled over 650,000 miles and carried 810,730 personnel. Refitted for commercial use.
1947	July 24	Left Southampton on mini cruise.
	July 31	Beginning of weekly service to New York with *Queen Elizabeth,* as originally planned kby Cunard White Star in 1930's. This service was maintained for next 20 years, though latterly at a loss.
1966		Due to development of jet air liners, *Queen Mary* now losing £750,000 per annum.
1967	September 22	Last crossing (1001st) from New York before being sold.
	October 31	Left Southampton for last voyage to new home in Long Beach, California.
	December 9	Arrived Long Beach, after 14,500 mile voyage.
1971		Hotel *Queen Mary* opened.

Appendix II

Captains of the Queen Mary

The following is a list of all Captains who have had command of the *Queen Mary*, with the date on which they first assumed command of the vessel.

Commodore Sir Edgar T. Britten, R.N.R.	1.12.35
Captain George Gibbons, C.B.E., R.D., R.N.R.	29.1.36
Commodore Reginald V. Peel, R.N.R.	4.8.36
Commodore Robert B. Irving, R.N.R.	11.11.36
Captain John C. Townley, R.N.R.	30.3.37
Captain Peter A. Murchie, R.N.R.	19.4.38
Captain Ernest M. Fall, C.B.E., D.S.C., R.D., R.N.R.	9.4.41
Commodore Sir James G.P. Bissett, C.B.E., R.D., R.N.R.	2.42
Captain Cyril G. Illingworth, R.D. R.N.R.	10.8.42
Captain Roland Spencer, R.D., R.N.R.	29.7.44
Commodore Chas. M. Ford, C.B.E., R.D., R.N.R.	11.3.46
Commodore George E. Cove	6.12.46
Commodore Sir C. Ivan Thompson	15.2.47
Captain John A. MacDonald, R.D., R.N.R.	6.3.47
Captain John D. Snow, R.D., R.N.R.	4.7.47
Commodore Harry Grattidge, O.B.E.	31.12.48
Captain Harry Dixon	20.7.50
Commodore Robert G. Thelwell	13.8.51
Captain Donald W. Sorrell	19.8.52
Commodore George G. Morris, C.B.E.	27.6.56
Commodore Chas. S. Williams	25.6.57
Captain Alexander B. Fasting, R.D., R.N.R.	11.9.57
Captain Andrew MacKellar, R.D., R.N.R.	26.8.58
Commodore John W. Caunce, R.D., R.N.R.	22.10.58
Commodore Donald M. MacLean, D.S.C., R.D., R.N.R.	24.6.59
Captain James Crosbie Dawson, D.S.C., R.D., R.N.R.	30.3.60
Captain Sidney A. Jones, R.D., R.N.R.	25.5.60
Commodore Frederick G. Watts, R.D., R.N.R.	9.8.60
Captain Eric A. Divers, C.B.E., R.D., R.N.R.	19.6.62
Commodore Geoffrey T. Marr, D.S.C., R.D., R.N.R.	7.5.64
Captain John Treasure Jones, R.D., R.N.R.	8.9.65
Captain William E. Warwick, R.D. R.N.R.	15.9.65
Captain William J. Law, R.D., R.N.R.	3.5.67

Appendix III

The Queen Mary's 1936 Log

The following information has been extracted from the ship' log covering her first 14 voyages in 1936, i.e. from the Maiden Voyage until Christmas. The route taken was in each case Southampton - Cherbourg - New York or vice versa. Abbreviations used are as follows:
P = Passengers. C = Crew. S = Stowaways.
Passage time given in Days - Hours - Minutes.
Speed given in knots.
B = Bullion or Specie carried as cargo.

Voyage	Dates	Captain	Passengers and Crew	Mileage	Passage Time	Average Speed
1W	27 May-1 Jun	Britten	1849-P 1186-C 2-S	3,158	4-12-24	29.13
			B = 82 boxes weighing 2 tons			
1E	5 Jun-10 Jun	Britten	1836-P 1203-C	3,198	4-15-15	28.74
2W	17 Jun-22 Jun	Britten		3,158	4-16-19	28.14
2E	24 Jun-29 Jun	Britten		3,198	4-15-18	28.73
3W	1 Jul-6 Jul	Britten		3,096	4-13-05	28.38
3E	8 Jul-13 Jul	Britten		3,129	4-14-15	28.38
	In King George V Graving Dock, Southampton: 14 - 19 July					
4W	22 Jul - 27 Jul	Britten		3,098	4-08-37	29.61
	First Record Voyage. Medical aid given by radio during crossing					
4E	29 Jul - 3 Aug	Britten		3,128	4-09-00	29.79
5W	5 Aug-10 Aug	Peel		3,087	4-14-31	27.96
5E	12 Aug-17 Aug	Peel		3,129	4-13-00	28.71
6W	19 Aug-24 Aug	Britten	1933-P 1213-C	3,097	4-04-12	30.01
	B = 9 boxes of gold, 504 bars of silver, total weight 17 tons					
6E	26 Aug-31 Aug	Britten	1437-P 1213-C 1-S	3,129	4-06-20	30.57
	Double Record Voyage					
7W	2 Sep-7 Sep	Britten	1925-P 1216-C	3,095	4-11-22	28.75
	B = 47 boxes of gold					
	Appendectomy successfully performed on crew member while at sea					
7E	9 Sep - 14 Sep	Britten	1358-P 1217-C 1-S	3,128	4-10-55	29.26
8W	16 Sep-21 Sep	Britten	1883-P 1219-C 1-S	3,097	4-14-53	27.93
	B = 58 boxes of gold					
8E	23 Sep-28 Sep	Britten	1548-P 1218-C	3,130	4-10-00	29.48

Voyage	Dates	Captain	Passengers and Crew	Mileage	Passage Time	Average Speed
9W	30 Sep-5 Oct	Britten	1814-P 1212-C	3,093	4-14-52	27.90
B = 416 bars of gold, 873 bars of silver, total weight 60 tons						
9E	7 Oct-12 Oct	Britten	1201-P 1211-C 1-S	3,130	4-10-24	29.41
10W	14 Oct-19 Oct	Peel	1640-P 1202-C	3,096	4-12-42	28.48
B = 44 boxes of gold, 1183 bars of silver, total weight 50 tons						
10E	21 Oct-26 Oct	Peel	1134-P 1201-C 1-S	3,129	4-16-24	27.84
11W	28 Oct-2 Nov	Peel	1518-P 1205-C	3,082	4-13-27	28.25
B = 168 boxes of gold, 137 bars of silver, total weight 10 tons.						
Commodore Britten had a stroke in his cabin 2 hours before sailing time. He died 5 hours later.						
11E	4 Nov-10 Nov	Peel	1201-P 1203-C Very rough seas	3,146	5-04-15	25.32
12W	11 Nov-17 Nov	Irving	983-P 1180-C Very rough seas	3,095	5-10-36	23.70
B = 62 boxes of gold, total weight 3 tons						
12E	18 Nov-23 Nov	Irving	977-P 1179-C	3,130	4-14-07	28.43
13W	25 Nov-30 Nov	Irving	1060-P 1189-C	3,096	4-13-27	28.29
13E	2 Dec-7 Dec	Irving	999-P 1189-C	3,132	4-13-57	28.49
14W	9 Dec-14 Dec	Peel	1084-P 1190-C	3,096	4-22-27	26.14
B = 26 boxes of gold, total weight 1 ton						
14E	16 Dec-22 Dec	Peel	1346-P 1189-C	3,129	5-01-12	25.73

Appendix IV

The Transatlantic Ferry

The following is a list of some of the many liners that have competed for the lucrative North Atlantic Ferry trade since a regular steamer service was inaugurated by Samuel Cunard in 1840. Tonnages are to the nearest 50 tons.

Year	Name	L.O.A. (feet)	Tonnage	
1840	*Britannia*	207	1100	
	Acadia			
	Caledonia			
	Columbia			
1848	'America' Class established by Samual Cunard			
1856	*Persia*			
1861	*Scotia*		3850	Last paddle steamer on Atlantic
1867	*Russia*	346	2950	
1871	*Oceanic*	420	3700	First White Star ship
	Baltic	420	3700	
	Republic	420	3700	Sister ships to *Oceanic*
	Adriatic	420	3600	
1872	*Cedric*			
1874	*Britannic*		5000	
	Germanic		5000	
1879	*Gallia*		4800	
1881	*Servia*			
1884	*Umbria*	519	8100	
	Etruria			Last ship with auxiliary sails
1891	*Furst Bismarck*	522	8450	
1893	*Lucania*		12950	
	Campania	622	12950	
1895	*St. Louis*	554	11250	Scrapped 1924
	St. Paul	554	11620	Scrapped 1923
1897	*Kaiser Wilhelm der Grosse*	655	14350	Scuttled 1914
1899	*Oceanic*	705	17250	Wrecked 1914
1901	*Celtic*	700	20900	
	Kronprinz Wilhelm	664	14900	Scrapped 1923
1903	*Carpathia*			Went to rescue of *Titanic*
	Cedric	700	21250	
	Kaiser Wilhelm II	709	19350	Record Holder. Scrapped 1940
1904	*Baltic*	726	23900	
1905	*Carmania*	675	20000	
1906	*Kaiserin Auguste Victoria*	705	24600	Later *Empress of Scotland* Destroyed by fire 1930.
1907	*Lusitania*	790	31550	Sunk 1915
	Mauretania	790	31950	Blue Riband Holder for 26 years. Scrapped 1935.
	Adriatic		24500	
	President Grant	616	18050	Later *Republic*. Scrapped 1951
1909	*George Washington*	723	25550	Destroyed by fire 1951
1911	*Olympic*	892	45350	Scrapped 1935
1912	*Titanic*	882	46300	Sunk 1912 on her maiden voyage
	France	713	23650	Scrapped 1934

1913	*Imperator*	919	52000	Later *Berengaria*. Scrapped 1938
1914	*Aquitania*	901	45650	Scrapped 1950
	Vaterland	948	54300	Later *Leviathan*. Scrapped 1938
1917	*Belgic*	696	27132	Later *Belgenland*. Scrapped 1936
1921	*Ausonia*	538	13900	Sister ships *Ascania* and *Andania*. Scrapped 1965
	Bismarck	954	56550	Later *Majestic*. Destroyed by fire 1939
	Paris	34550		Destroyed by fire
1922	*Andania*	538	13950	Scrapped 1961
	Homeric	774	34350	Scrapped 1936
	Montrose	575	16400	Scrapped 1952
	Pennland	600	16350	Sunk 1941
	Lone Star State	535	14200	Later *President Harding*. Destroyed by fire 1940
1923	*Ascania*	538	14000	Scrapped 1956
	Albert Ballin	627	20800	Scrapped 1981
	Ohio	615	18950	Scrapped 1934
1924	*Columbus*	775	32350	Scuttled 1939
	Deutschland	627	20600	Sunk during WWII
1925	*Gripsholm*	573	18000	Later *Berlin*. Scrapped 1966
1926	*Hamburg*	635	21150	Scrapped 1977
1927	*Isle de France*		43150	
	New York	635	21,450	Sunk 1945
1929	*Bremen*	938	51750	Blue Riband Holder. Destroyed by fire 1941
	Milwaukee	575	16700	Scrapped 1952
1930	*Britannic*	712	26950	Scrapped 1961
	Europa	941	49750	Blue Riband Holder. Scrapped 1962
	Empress of Japan	666	26050	Name changed during WWII to *Empress of Scotland*. Damaged by fire and scrapped 1966
1931	*Empress of Britain*	760	42350	Sunk 1940
1932	*Georgic*	711	27750	Scrapped 1956
	Manhattan	705	24300	Scrapped 1965
	Rex		51050	Blue Riband Holder 1933. Sunk 1944
1932	*Conte di Savoia*		48500	Sunk 1943
1935	*Normandie*	1029	79300	Blue Riband Holder. Destroyed by fire 1942
1936	*Queen Mary*	1018	80750	Blue Riband Holder
	Batory	526	14300	Scrapped 1971
1938	*Nieuw Amsterdam*	758	36300	Scrapped 1974
1939	*Mauretania*	772	35400	Scrapped 1965
1940	*Queen Elizabeth*	1035	83650	Destroyed by fire 1972
1946	*America*	723	33550	
1948	*Caronia*	715	34200	Sank 1974
1952	*United States*	990	53350	Last Blue Riband Holder
	Stefan Batory	503	15000	
1954	*Saxonia*	608	21650	Later *Carmania*
1955	*Ivernia*	608	21700	Sister ship to *Saxonia*, *Sylvania*, and *Carinthia*
1956	*Carinthia*	608	21950	
1957	*Statendam*	642	24300	
1959	*Rotterdam*	748	38650	
	Bremen	697	29250	Originally *Pasteur* 1939. Sank on way to Breakers 1980
1961	*France*	1035	66350	
1969	*Queen Elizabeth 2*	963	65850	

Index